Practice

KEYWORDS IN TEACHER EDUCATION

Series Editor: Viv Ellis

Taking cultural theorist Raymond Williams's concept as an organizing device, the **Keywords in Teacher Education** series offers short, accessibly written books on the most pressing and challenging ideas in the field.

Teacher education has a high profile in public policy and professional debates given the enduring associations between how teachers are prepared and how well their students do in school. At the same time, research perspectives on the important topics in the field are increasingly polarized with important consequences for the kind of teacher and the qualities of teaching that are most valued. Written by internationally recognized experts, these titles offer analyses both of the historical emergence and the consequences of the different positions in these debates.

Also Available in the Series:

Knowledge, Steven Puttick, Victoria Elliott and Jenni Ingram
Disadvantage, Jo Lampert, Jane Wilkinson, Mervi Kaukko and Rocío García-Carrión
Communities, Kenneth M. Zeichner
Identity, Sarah Steadman
Quality, Clare Brooks
Expertise, Jessica Gerrard and Jessica Holloway

Practice
Keywords in Teacher Education

KATHERINE SCHULTZ
AND
RACHEL THROOP

BLOOMSBURY ACADEMIC
LONDON • NEW YORK • OXFORD • NEW DELHI • SYDNEY

BLOOMSBURY ACADEMIC
Bloomsbury Publishing Plc, 50 Bedford Square, London, WC1B 3DP, UK
Bloomsbury Publishing Inc, 1359 Broadway, New York, NY 10018, USA
Bloomsbury Publishing Ireland, 29 Earlsfort Terrace, Dublin 2, D02 AY28, Ireland

BLOOMSBURY, BLOOMSBURY ACADEMIC and the Diana logo are trademarks of Bloomsbury Publishing Plc

First published in Great Britain 2026

Cover design by Charlotte James
Cover image © Zoonar GmbH / Alamy Stock Photo

A catalogue record for this book is available from the British Library.
A catalog record for this book is available from the Library of Congress.

ISBN: HB: 978-1-3505-4317-1
PB: 978-1-3505-4316-4
ePDF: 978-1-3505-4318-8
eBook: 978-1-3505-4319-5

Series: Keywords in Teacher Education

Typeset by Newgen KnowledgeWorks Pvt. Ltd., Chennai, India
Printed and bound in Great Britain

For product safety related questions contact productsafety@bloomsbury.com.

To find out more about our authors and books visit www.bloomsbury.com and sign up for our newsletters.

For our children: Nora, Danny, and Jenna & Samir and Maya, who we imagine will continue to invent new practices that will shape our future.

CONTENTS

SERIES EDITOR'S FOREWORD

This series is organized by the concept of "keywords," first elaborated by Welsh cultural theorist Raymond Williams (1976), and books in the series will seek to problematize and unsettle the ostensibly unproblematic and settled vocabulary of teacher education. From Williams's perspective, keywords are words and phrases that occur frequently in speech and writing, allowing conversation to ensue, but that nonetheless reveal profound differences in meaning within and across cultures, politics, and histories. In teacher education, such keywords include practice, knowledge, quality, and expertise. The analysis of such keywords allows us to trace the evolution of the emergent—and the maintenance of residual—meanings in teacher education discourses and practices. By analyzing keywords, therefore, it is possible to elucidate the range of meanings of what Gallie (1955) referred to as "essentially contested concepts" but in ways that promote a critical, historical understanding of changes in the fields in which they occur.

In the first edition of *Keywords*, Williams included entries on 108 units, ranging from "Aesthetic" to "Work." A second edition followed in 1983, and other writers have subsequently used the concept to expand on Williams's original collection (e.g., Bennett et al., 2005; MacCabe and Yanacek, 2018) or to apply the concept to specific domains (e.g., A Community of Inquiry, 2018). This series applies it to teacher education. The purpose of the series mirrors that of Williams's original project: to trace ideological differences and social conflicts over time as they relate to the discourses and practices of a field (here, teacher education) by focusing on a selection of the field's high-frequency words. So *Keywords in Teacher Education* is not a multivolume dictionary. Each book will explore a critically important issue in teacher education by interrogating one significant lexical item in its vocabulary.

The kind of analysis required by a focus on keywords goes beyond etymology or historical semantics. By selecting and analyzing keywords, Williams argued:

> We find a history and complexity of meanings; conscious changes, or consciously different uses; innovation, obsolescence, specialization, extension, overlap, transfer; or changes which are masked by a nominal continuity so that words which seem to have been there for centuries, with continuous general meanings, have come in fact to express radically different or radically variable, yet sometimes hardly noticed, meanings and implications of meaning. (Williams, 1976, p. 17)

Given the increasingly strong attention given to teacher education in education policy and in public debates about education more generally, focusing on keywords in this field is both timely and necessary. Uncovering and unsettling differences and conflicts in the vocabulary of preparing teachers renders the political and social bases underlying policy formation and public discourse more visible and therefore more capable of being acted upon.

Through this organizing device, the *Keywords in Teacher Education* series addresses the most important topics and questions in teacher education currently. It is a series of short books written in a direct and accessible style, each book taking one keyword as its point of departure and closely examining its cultural meanings historically while, crucially, identifying the social force and material consequences of the differences and conflicts in meaning. Written by internationally recognized researchers, each peer-reviewed book offers cutting-edge analysis of the keyword underpinned by a deep knowledge of the available research within the field—and beyond it. One of the aims of the series is to broaden the gaze of teacher education research by engaging more systematically with the relevant humanities and social science literature—to acknowledge, as Williams did, that our understanding is deepened and potential for action strengthened by seeking to understand the social relations between words, texts, and the multiple contexts in which their meanings are produced.

In this wonderful contribution to the Keywords series, Katherine Schultz and Rachel Throop have provided a careful explication of the contexts and contours of debates about the meanings of practice in teacher education. They begin by showing just how polysemic a word practice is, especially in a field like teacher education, where it is woven into almost every aspect of our everyday understandings. Schultz and Throop are especially good at clarifying the distinctions between sometimes conflicting or contradictory meanings while also taking the heat out of the debates, something that has characterized discussion of practice, "core practices," and "practice-based" in the pages of journals and on the conference floor. They are also very successful at identifying what is at stake in these debates about the meanings of practice in teacher education—the aims of education, specifically the goals of educational and social justice and tackling inequitable outcomes. Not that any one side of these debates outright rejects tackling inequity or doesn't think that the concept of justice is irrelevant to teacher preparation. Rather, different sides have different ideas as to how they might be achieved and/or have different definitions or have a different priority for them. And, of course, different meanings of and purposes for practice.

The authors also clearly identify how marketization and privatization have impacted the practices of teacher education in what has become something of a battle for the meaning of practice. Short-circuiting the development of teaching expertise through the specification of certain behaviors or actions, supported by resources, and "rehearsed" with fidelity, is a process that has become ripe for capitalization. However, such an approach (which may or may not be consonant with the dominant definitions of "practice-based teacher education") is also an approach that centers on control of the teacher—and the teacher educator. So while marketization and privatization are clearly highly relevant, we have also more recently been reminded that conservatism, traditionalism, or even far-right white nationalism have also had an impact on the political and policy-level discourses of teacher education—and the funding of institutions (Ellis, Gatti, and Mansell, 2024).

This book is also extremely helpful in at least one other way: for highlighting the way in which what was predominantly a concern of policymakers, researchers, and practitioners in the United States has driven an agenda across research and policy around the world. The (re)turn to practice, the notion of "core practices," "practice-based teacher education" emerged in the United States in a context where there had been concerns about the fragmentation of the country's teacher education programs (distributed across different departments of the university as well as schools) as well as limited opportunities to teach on school placements in addition to concerns about an overly theoretical or reflective (often defined as "navel-gazing") curriculum in universities. While this may or may not have been true in the United States, it certainly wasn't in many other places. In England, to give two examples, the systemic concerns "and risks might have been identified very differently: very long (by international standards) school placements and lots of "practice teaching" with hit-and-miss mentoring; and overreliance on one teacher educator (especially in graduate-level secondary programs) who teach pretty much everything to the student teacher in the same university classroom every week when they are not in school. Even a key phrase in the US-centric discourse—"teacher of record"—has no meaning—or different meanings—in other national contexts. Yet the global energy around the keyword practice, the questions asked, and the "solutions" proposed took hold in often not very productive ways, deflecting attention from local contexts, needs, and priorities. Practice and the very notion of practice as a keyword in teacher education owes its energy to the dominance of US-centric research and policy discourses.

This volume in the Keywords series also makes another very important contribution through the interviews with leading researchers that the authors have conducted for this book and that appear in Chapter 4. The interview with Marilyn Cochran-Smith is especially useful in helping to clarify nuances in the meanings of practice and practice-based—particularly in noting the distinction between merely "being in a school" and participating in a practice. Cochran-Smith, like Schulz and Throop, ultimately proposes a strongly sociocultural and anthropological understanding of practice. Practice—the practice of teaching—is a context-specific human activity undertaken with some conceptual and material tools that have been shaped historically and that is directed at more or less shared educational and social goals. That is what makes teaching and teacher education so recognizable, important, complex, but absolutely achievable. Schulz and Throop's contribution to the Keywords series opens up a new space for thinking about practice and what is both possible and desirable.

Viv Ellis
London, 2026

ACKNOWLEDGMENTS

Our deep appreciation for Thea Abu El-Haj and Rebecca Steinitz who each read many versions of the proposal. To Ken Zeichner, whose sage advice, connections, and book, *Communities*, got us started on this project. To Lin Goodwin, Misty Sato, and Rachel Lotan for kindly reaching out to their international colleagues to ask about "practices." To Pam Grossman, Lani Horn, Megan Franke, Urban Fraefel, Kirsti Klette, Inga Jenset, and Marilyn Cochran-Smith who generously added their wisdom and vast knowledge on this topic. To Shreya Sunderram, Erica Harreveld, Nicki Felmus, and Ishrat Ahmed whose perspectives on practice enriched our thinking. Finally, to Viv Ellis, who coached us at the beginning and inspired us throughout the writing of the book.

CHAPTER 1

Practice as a Keyword in Teacher Education

As a thought experiment, describe teaching without focusing on people (the teacher or the students). The end result might be considered a practice based on action (e.g., to achieve a quiet classroom, count to ten) or a discursive strategy (e.g., begin your lecture with an overview of the topic). Alternatively, you might choose to describe a practice that is more complex, involving several steps (e.g., to hold a discussion, begin by arranging the seating in the classroom).

Ask any educator, though, and they will tell you that once you try to implement these practices in a classroom, things rarely go as planned. Teachers understand that it isn't useful to imagine teaching solely as a practice that occurs in a vacuum. Teaching is more than a set of strategies that lead to higher test scores or the attainment of a skill; while it might be convenient to imagine that teaching is this simple, doing so is rarely useful to classroom teachers. To discuss practice in a way that is useful to the profession, we must start from the assumption that teaching practices are intrinsically connected to both the teacher and student, as well as the context. As we consider a teacher's practice, we take into account—among other things—what the teacher knows, their prior experiences, their stance, their dispositions, their understanding of history and context, and their ability to respond to students. Further, we consider the students, their prior knowledge and experiences, their context, and their willingness to learn. Finally, we make explicit the give-and-take that exceptional educators often act on intuitively; teaching and learning are reciprocal, and teachers learn from students at the same time students learn from teachers. Teaching is not simply a decontextualized strategy, it includes—indeed, it centers on, in bell hooks' (1984, p. 175) words—"being with people."

Practice as a Keyword

The books in this series draw on the work of Raymond Williams and his concept of "keywords" (1976). For Williams, keywords were significant and often contested words whose meanings changed according to the social, political, and economic moment. Commenting on Williams's thesis, Leary (2022) explains that keywords are those words that "contain and constrain certain forms of thought" (p. 8); in other words, they help create the boundaries for what we imagine as possible. The flip side of this, of course, is that by identifying and interrogating keywords, we have a "key," that can help us to unlock the bind that these keywords place us in (Leary, 2018, 2022); if we can open up keywords, it helps us to imagine different ways of acting and engaging. This book situates the word "practice" in this tradition.

There is substantive debate about practice and its meanings within the university-based teacher education community. We discuss the contours of this debate in this chapter and the chapters that follow. We also look beyond this debate to other, arguably more consequential areas where different understandings of practice are defined and mobilized to shape global policy agendas. Notions of best practices, for example, have paved the way for teacher accountability efforts and school privatization initiatives; teacher educators rarely have input in these conversations, even as they dramatically shape the contexts we are preparing teachers for.

One key contribution this book aims to make is to show how actors who are not directly involved in the preparation of teachers—state regulatory boards, iNGOs, business leaders, and philanthropists, for example—use discourses of practice to shape policy and limit teacher autonomy. As these efforts feed marketization and privatization efforts, teacher educators see their voice and power becoming more and more limited. An interrogation of practice shows that, despite more minor internal disagreement around practice in the teacher education community, there is much commonality and shared interest when we place conversations about practice into a broader context. Interrogating practice makes clear the stakes and the urgency in reclaiming the discourse around practice and asserting our expertise. As teacher educators, this is a concept we need to claim as our domain.

For Williams, exploring keywords is not an intellectual exercise; the aim is to uncover and address inequality. This book suggests that interrogating and debating practice helps teacher educators gain the edge that Williams argues is so critical for responding to inequity and opening up new futures and new possibilities. It is easy to despair when we think about educational privatization efforts globally that put profits ahead of learning, or when we consider the ways teachers are de-professionalized and limited by accountability regimes. If we look clearly and honestly at these shifts in the global educational landscape, however, we can consider them not with panic but with possibility. We can think about how to redirect these shifts toward a radically different, progressive future. There are, of course, many ways to do this critical work. In this book, we suggest that interrogating, engaging, and reclaiming practice, as well as initiating dialogue across different stakeholder groups and people holding different understandings, offer one especially productive route.

Stakeholders in Conversations About Practice

In writing this book, we considered three distinct groups that have consequential conversations about teachers' practice: policymakers, teacher educators, and teachers themselves. Several of these conversations overlap, while others are more distinct. For example, many teacher educators work closely with teachers at all different phases in their careers; both groups learn from each other in ways that, ideally, shape their practices and how they understand those practices. In contrast, policymakers rarely have substantive conversations with classroom teachers or teacher educators, even as some of their ideas may end up being taken up in policy. One aim for this book is to look across the various conversations about practice, including areas of disagreement, in order to promote understandings of practice that constructively shape teacher education programs across the globe.

On a global scale, educational policy conversations about practice are often framed around best practices or core practices. When a practice is labeled as best or core, it seems to offer an unquestionable good. When we interrogate the uses of "practice" in these conversations, however, we see that discourses of practice are often used as a way to gain control over teachers and teacher education, often sidelining questions of teacher professionalism and autonomy. In recent years, teacher education has increasingly come under scrutiny; as teachers are positioned as key to improving education around the globe, teacher education has become central to educational policymaking efforts. Governmental and nongovernmental policymakers imagine that shifting teacher education can elevate the overall standard of education, improve schools, and increase student achievement (e.g., Furlong et al., 2000). Teacher educators and teachers are rarely a part of these conversations, even as they have crucial knowledge of content, teaching, students, and are often positioned as the key lever to increasing student achievement. Controlling teacher practices in the interest of raising test scores is too often the goal of educational policy.

We see different conversations happening amongst teacher educators. Teacher educators talk about practice in a range of ways including conversations around practice teaching and communities of practice. One of the richest debates in the field over recent years has been the debate around core practices and high leverage practices. These are practices, drawn from observations of classrooms, that teacher education scholars explain are critical for learning to teach. They are generally broken into component parts so that they are easier to teach and learn and are found in teacher education programs around the world. As we detail below, and in the chapters that follow, teacher educators also talk about the role of practice in teacher education, often labeling programs as practice-based teacher education.

We can also think about conversations around or understandings of practice as they circulate among teachers themselves. Lortie (1975) wrote many years ago about the apprenticeship of observation, demonstrating that many teachers fall back on the teaching practices they experienced or were taught as students. In other words, their many years as students in classrooms often take precedence over the methods they learn in their preparation programs. More recently, teachers have been drawn to a popular website Teachers Pay Teachers (TPT) where, according to the TPT company, over seven million teachers have downloaded more than a billion resources (Swalwell et al., 2023). While there are numerous critiques of the low quality of these materials (Swalwell et al., 2023), there is no doubt that it feeds conversations about teaching practice among teachers.

An alternative to this phenomenon is found in the conversations of practice that occur when teachers gather in learning communities, both formal and informal, to exchange practices and support for each other to address the current issues they face in their classrooms. A stunning example of this is when teachers use descriptive practices, including the "Descriptive Review of a Child" (e.g., Carini, 1986). This set of practices was developed by Patricia Carini and her colleagues at the Prospect Archive and Center for Education and Research to focus on a single child and their strengths and interests, teachers' questions about their own pedagogical practices, as well as larger issues of classroom practice. Teachers use this set of practices as a way to address a focusing question such as: How can I engage this child who appears to be resistant to learning mathematical algorithms? It is a set of practices that invites all of the teachers into the conversation and, in turn, informs each of the teacher's practice when they return to their classrooms. Practice, in this sense, is deeply connected to their knowledge of students, including the students' experiences and understandings, interests, and dispositions. In these conversations, practice isn't a singular way of enacting a strategy or set of moves; it is intimately tied to learning and community.

Meanings of Practice in Teacher Education

The meanings of practice both vary and remain constant across stakeholders. Practice is a word that is used across professions and activities. We talk about a doctor's practice, a contemplative practice, and also a teaching practice. At times, practice connotes an organized set of knowledge, accepted ways of enacting activities, or a group of people who work together. Scholars and educators often write about practice in contrast to theory, with practice more connected to action and theory connected to the beliefs or logics behind those actions. A teaching practice includes both what is taught and how it is taught.

We find anthropological lenses on teaching and learning useful when thinking about definitions of practice. While practices are often thought of as formulas for action, devoid of context, they are better understood as complex activities located in a specific place and time, encompassing larger purposes and histories. We argue that practices are more than just what teachers do (Holland et al., 1998), and are different and more complex than events (Street, 2001). Individuals don't simply invent practices; practices emerge in social interaction and are dependent on the historical contexts from which they emerge (Scribner and Cole 1981). Practices can circulate, but different communities of practice will make and (re)make them over time (Lave, 1991). Anthropologists define learning as social practice, suggesting that learning involves the transformation of practices that, in turn, change in response to the learner (Lave, 1991). Learning to teach doesn't happen in a single place or time, but over time and across contexts. In the process, both the learning and the person learning to teach are transformed.

Practice is a common word in teacher education. At times it is taken for granted, while at other times it is highly contested. Practices can be used to describe the everyday actions of teachers. They can be used to mandate and control teachers' actions, leaving little room for choice and judgment, or they can be a space for opportunity and growth. At times, practices become the central activities of teacher education programs. Too often, the practices involved in becoming a teacher are conceptualized as if those practices are separate from the teacher or the students. If we conceptualize teaching as "being with people" as hooks (1994, p. 175) suggests, then practices must be considered through this same lens, as intrinsically linked to teachers and teaching.

In their exploration of the relationships between knowledge and practice in teacher learning, Cochran-Smith and Lytle (1999) propose an important set of distinctions that can operate as a framework for understanding practice: knowledge *of* practice, which generally comes from university-based research; knowledge *in* practice or practical knowledge and the knowledge that is derived from teachers' work; and knowledge *for* practice or knowledge teachers gain when they engage in practitioner research to investigate their own practice by taking an inquiry stance. Cochran-Smith and Lytle (1999, pp. 290–1) explain further:

> From the perspective of inquiry as stance, however, neither the activity of teaching nor inquiry about teaching are captured by the notion that practice is practical. Rather, teaching and thus teacher learning are centrally about forming and re-forming frameworks for understanding practice: how students and their teachers construct the curriculum, co-mingling their experiences, their cultural and linguistic resources, and their interpretive frameworks; how teachers' actions are infused with complex and multilayered understandings of learners, culture, class, gender, literacies, social issues, institutions, histories, communities, materials, texts, and curricula; and how teachers work together to develop and alter their questions and interpretive frameworks informed not only by thoughtful consideration of the immediate situation and the particular students they teach and have taught but also by the multiple contexts within which they work.

Taking an inquiry stance toward practice allows teachers to interrogate and interpret the meanings of practice as they learn how to teach.

We turn now to four common and consequential uses of the word practice in the field of education generally and teacher preparation more specifically, in order to further delineate the uses of the word practice in teacher education. We begin with a discussion of practice teaching, which is ubiquitous around the world and often known as clinical practice. We next turn to practice-based teacher education or placing practice at the center of learning to teach. A recent set of ideas known as "core practices" or "high leverage practices" has become popular in the United States and taken up around the globe. This set of ideas, grounded in the practice-based teacher education movement, seeks to identify key strategies teachers need to learn to become successful in the classroom. A related use of practice is "best practices," a more generic term that is used across disciplines, originating in the business world and migrating to fields like social work, nursing, and education. We consider how the designation of teaching practices as "best practices" has enabled them to be replicated or scaled and spread across the globe.

Each of these understandings of practice is critical for exploring the role of practice in teacher education. As we elaborate in subsequent chapters, practice is a term whose meaning is often unquestioned and underexplored, yet it has significant implications for how teacher education programs are structured, including the focus of the courses and clinical experiences.

Practice Teaching

An important aspect of learning to teach is practice teaching or learning to teach in classrooms in partnership with current teachers. Across the world, practice teaching, student teaching, or clinical preparation is commonly understood as connecting the more theoretical knowledge taught at the university with practical knowledge and experience in classrooms (e.g., Anderson and Stillman, 2013; Darling-Hammond, 2017). Practice teaching is often conceptualized as a time and place to practice what is learned in the university classroom; through practice, teachers often learn from the teachers whose classrooms are their sites of practice. Dresden and Thompson (2021, p. 10) pose the following definition of clinical practice:

> Rather, we view clinical practice as that space in which TCs [teacher candidates] are given opportunities to see the reality of classroom life and are supported by their mentors to notice small, perhaps hidden, actions, emotions, and expressions of thought and feeling. In clinical practice, theory and practice do not cohabit while maintaining their

> own distinct identities; rather, clinical practice is the place TCs can "interrogate [both theory and practice] in light of the other."
>
> (Burn and Mutton, 2015, p. 219)

They argue further that well-designed and carefully supervised clinical practice experiences can break down the divide between theory and practice (Dresden and Thompson, 2021).

The location, length, and quality of clinical placements vary across the world and have changed over time. For instance, in the 1980s, there was a movement in England to relocate 80 percent of teaching preparation from the university to school-based programs (Goodson, 1993). In Finland, the clinical preparation of teachers occurs in teacher training schools that are overseen by the universities. Teachers in these schools are carefully selected for their expertise and expected to participate in professional learning and engage in research in conjunction with the Department of Teacher Education. Similar partnerships between universities and schools occur in Australia, Canada, and Singapore (Darling-Hammond, 2017). There is great variation in the length of student teaching, often connected to both the attention to practice in the teacher education program and also the amount of continuing education expected once students enter classrooms. In Japan, for instance, student teaching is just two to four weeks long, with extensive professional development built around the practice of Lesson Study during a teachers' initial years of teaching (Lewis, 2010). In contrast, there are yearlong clinical placements with intensive supervision and learning opportunities in many parts of Western Europe and the United States.

There are variations in the length of time set aside for student teaching, as well, in fast-track alternative programs like Teach for America in the United States and derivative programs such as Teach for All in other parts of the world. For example, in Teach for America, new teachers become the teacher of record after a brief, usually six-week long, student teaching period in a summer school classroom (Zeichner, 2021). In contrast, residency programs often have longer periods of student teaching where prospective teachers gradually take on classroom responsibilities over the course of a full school year (Gatti, 2019; Solomon, 2009).

The physician Atul Gawande (2002) posed the question of whether doctors (and by extension teachers) should learn a practice on actual patients (students) who may be put in harm's way, ultimately concluding that repeated practice in real settings is necessary to gain fluency and expertise. To address this dilemma, teacher educators have developed simulations and incorporated videotaping and rehearsals into university classrooms, even using avatars in place of actual students for practicing in online environments (e.g., Cohen et al., 2020; Kim, 2024). Bringing student teaching into the university classroom allows the student teacher to focus on learning the designated practice rather than managing people and the environment. Ball and Forzani (2009) use the term "designed setting" to suggest a context for learning to teach that would "eliminate or reduce the need for students to engage with some aspects of the work of teaching while focusing attention on particular parts of the work" (p. 504). Proponents argue that this allows prospective teachers to practice without concern that they will harm children or slow down children's learning. Their decisions can be observed, discussed, and critiqued. While this may work for learning some aspects of teaching before entering the classroom, we wonder what is missing when context is stripped away and the relationships at the heart of teaching are removed. This seems to undermine the basic concept that teaching is essentially about interactions with people and managing complexity.

Practice-Based Teacher Education

The term "practice-based teacher education" has recently become central to global conversations about learning to teach. This movement places practice, rather than theory, at the center of teacher education, inviting teacher educators to focus their coursework on practice in order to increase congruence between the university and the field (cf., Matsumoto-Royo and Ramírez-Montoya 2021; McDonald et al., 2013). Practice-based courses are taught by university instructors, classroom teachers, and even community-based educators (Zeichner et al., 2023). The core practice or high-leverage practice movement, described in the next section, was introduced in the United States and designed to improve teacher preparation through the identification of key practices that all prospective teachers should learn and use. The scholars working within this framework wanted to further elaborate practice-based teacher education and sought to create a common vocabulary of practice through this work, which has spread to many parts of the world (e.g., Grossman and Fraefel, 2024).

Programs that are practice-based may be located in either the university or the schools. However, as Zeichner (2012) explains, the physical location of a teacher education course does not necessarily make it practice based. In recent years "'clinically rich' or 'clinically-oriented' teacher preparation has become the new slogan in the field and significant national reform efforts based on this concept have emerged" (Zeichner, 2018, p. 5).

One unintended result of the move to make teacher education more practice-focused in Britain, locating it in schools rather than the university, was the disappearance of a focus on the social, political, historical, and cultural issues of education from the curriculum (Whitty et al., 2007). As Zeichner (2018) explains, "shifting teacher education to be more school based without building the capacity in schools for handling their increased role in initial teacher preparation will result in a situation like that which occurred in the UK where a shift to school-based preparation merely served to reproduce the status quo" (p. 31). Ellis and McNicholl (2015) elaborate further that "the practices of teacher education as a field afford and constrain different kinds of development for teachers" (p. 9). As a result, simply bringing practices from the classroom to the university isn't sufficient for learning to teach.

Adding decision-making, reflection, improvisation strategies, and judgment is essential, as is taking an inquiry stance.

Core Practices

The "core practices" or "high leverage practices" movement (e.g., Ball and Forzani, 2009; Grossman, 2018) grows out of the turn toward practice-based teacher education and is conceptualized as a set of principled activities that are shaped by the contexts in which they are enacted through improvisation and adaptation (Grossman, 2018; Lampert et al., 2013). In response to the call for changing how prospective teachers learn to teach and ensuring that teachers are better equipped to implement practices in their first years in the classroom, teacher education scholars have sought to identify the essential practices a prospective teacher needs to learn. Locating their work in the Core Practices Consortium and TeachingWorks, two collections of resources that emphasize equity and practice-based approaches, teacher educators developed core practices to support teachers to integrate a theoretically informed skills-based approach with the pedagogical knowledge of how to enact those practices in a flexible manner. Some examples of core practices include implementing strategies and routines that are connected to disciplinary learning, leading discussions, and eliciting and responding to students' ideas (Ball and Forzani, 2009; Grossman, et al., 2018; Lampert et al., 2013). The core practice movement has spread internationally. As McDonald (2013) and colleagues explain,

> by highlighting specific, routine aspects of teaching that demand the exercise of professional judgment and the creation of meaningful intellectual and social community for teachers, teacher educators, and students, core practices may offer teacher educators powerful tools for preparing teachers for the constant in-the-moment decision-making that the profession requires.
>
> (p. 378)

Critics of this movement argue that core practices don't address key equity issues in classrooms because they fail to attend to the specific and situated nature of teaching and the political and economic moment (Philip et al., 2019; Daniels and Varghese, 2019). Philip and his colleagues (2019) advocate for criticality about how core practices are tied to market-based reform measures in teacher education. They argue that the push toward prioritizing the knowledge and practices of dominant groups in a quest toward improving student achievement obscures the humanizing potential of public education. Ellis and Orchard (2014) explain that high leverage practices are often prioritized by schools and systems in order to promote particular outcomes such as higher test scores. They argue that high leverage or core practices have become "highly prized within the value-system of teacher education reform" and are often positioned "in distinction to (or even in opposition to) theory, reflection or deliberative discourse of any kind" (p. 2).

Best Practices

Another common way we see the language of practice used in teacher education is through the discourse of best practices. The concept of best practices originated in the business world and quickly spread to educational circles, becoming shorthand for practice-based interventions that are imagined to increase student achievement. Unlike "core practices," which are derived from academic debate and are rooted in research, "best practices" is a more ambiguous term. In recent years, some education scholars have replaced the language of best practices with promising practices, as a way of acknowledging that no single practice is best in all contexts. While this is productive, the discourse of best practices persists. At first glance, it is hard to argue with best practices: they have a built-in self-justifying logic. As we argue here, however, the discourse of best practices is about much more than what works in the classroom.

One key—and often overlooked—function the discourse of best practices serves is to fuel global policy spread. In recent years, teacher education has become central to educational policy conversations. We once thought of educational policy as traveling between bounded nation-states; in a globalized world, however, this isn't the best way to think about policy spread. A more useful lens is to think about shared orientations. Scholars in the field of comparative educational research have explicitly made this argument, calling for attention to trends "like the orientation to 'best practices' " (Steiner-Khamsi, 2021, p. 339). Governments, iNGOs, and other extra-governmental bodies craft policies that promote what they consider to be "best practices." Various venues, such as independent graduate schools in the United States, also do this in their own ways. As a result, we increasingly see coherence in teaching practices across the globe. These practices are often divorced from theory and educational research and devoid of context. They are also deeply intertwined with marketization and privatization efforts.

In conjunction with and beyond global policy spread, discourses of best practice have multiple functions and uses. Increasingly, we see models of teaching spreading globally that are justified by and employ a singular, scripted version of "best practice" (Ball, 2012; Steiner-Khamsi, 2021). Philanthropists and education entrepreneurs use the language of best practices to signal their membership in the educational community and gain traction for their ideas. Just as the discourse of best practices paves the way for voices outside the educational community to claim expertise, it also works to naturalize the idea that market logic should drive educational systems worldwide. Additionally, the discourse is deployed to support scaling of international models that position the learning and growth of children as secondary to goals of profit. Inherent in the discourse of "best practices" is a mechanism for sidestepping accountability. On a global scale, the idea of best practices has become aligned with ideas around maximizing profits and prioritizing scalability;

this undermines democracy as it forecloses local control and shuts out local stakeholders (Hook, 2021; Verger et al., 2016). We discuss these ideas further in Chapter 3, arguing for the importance of bringing versions of these conversations into teacher education programs.

Chapter Overview

In this book, our focus is on the multiple meanings of practice in teaching and learning to teach. We argue that a deeper understanding of what is meant by practice should inform the design of teacher education programs, prompt productive conversations across typical divides, as well as inform decisions made by policymakers that shape teaching across the world. We understand practice as inseparable from people, places, and time. Lave (2012, p. 157) asks: "How are lives, persons, and practices produced in ongoing everyday practice?" We wonder, more specifically, how the practices of learning to teach shape and are shaped by prospective teachers, teacher educators, and teachers.

Chapter 2 provides a historical overview of how practice-based teaching has been defined and implemented around the world. We examine how ideas about practice in teacher education have changed over time. Finally, we look at how groups of people have developed teacher education programs in response to the perceived global crisis in education by relying on limited understandings and uses of practice.

Chapter 3 explores the way the discourse of "best practices" promotes the spread of global policy and feeds marketization trends. We look across national contexts through two case studies—low fee private schools (LFPS) in Kenya and charter schools in the US city of New Orleans—to demonstrate how reliance on discourses of best practices shift the terrain of educational policy and fuel marketization and privatization efforts. We consider the consequences for teachers' work, arguing that a critical interrogation of practice can help resist the ways in which impoverished notions of practice undermine teaching and learning.

Chapter 4 draws on interviews with scholars who have written extensively about practice to explore how their understandings of practice have led to design decisions for teacher education programs. We look for the commonalities across their understandings, highlighting the robust ideas of practice and complex notions of teachers' work that all of the scholars share. Building on this, we ask what it would mean to support dialogue in place of conflict as a source for reimagining teacher education.

Conclusion: The Importance of Interrogating the Meanings of Practice

Our review of the meanings and uses of practice in teacher education leads us to the conclusion that it is vital that we engage in conversations about practice across various stakeholder groups, while always valuing and foregrounding the perspectives of practicing teachers. Dialogue is critical so that education does not become a site for political battles and profit, which leads to impoverished understandings of teacher education, teachers, and teaching. We believe that this exploration of the word practice might lead to productive conversations that inform the structure and basis of teacher education programs, allowing teacher educators to ground their work in deeper understandings and assert their expertise around practice.

To this end, we ask: How can those of us who are directly involved in the preparation and support of teachers act to transform teacher education, centering complex notions of practice that honor teachers' work? How can a historical understanding of practice inform the present, taking into account the political, social, and economic forces that shape the decisions and trends? How can we challenge the ways that marketization efforts shape global education policy, limiting teacher autonomy and undermining robust student learning? And, how can interrogating and challenging some of the dominant meanings of the word practice—particularly the impoverished notions of practice becoming increasingly common across the globe—help us to do this?

CHAPTER 2

A History of Practice in Teacher Education

Scholars trace the current turn toward practice in teacher education to an article written by Ball and Cohen (1999) that urged teacher educators to identify the central practices of classroom teaching in order to prepare prospective teachers (Forzani, 2014; Zeichner, 2012). The article was intended to reshape teachers' professional education, anchoring it in the idea of learning *in* and *from* practice (Feiman-Nemser and Remillard, 1996). Ball and Cohen (1999) suggested that through artifacts such as videos of teaching and learning, as well as other records of practice such as students' work, teachers could learn from practice in both the university classroom and their field placements.

The move toward emphasizing practice in teacher education is understood as a way to address the problem that university-based teacher education is often too theoretical and removed from classroom practice, what Feiman-Nemser and Buchmann (1985) called the "two worlds pitfall" (cf., Braaten, 2018; Payne et al., 2025). This refers to the sometimes unbridged distance between what is taught in university classrooms and what teachers actually do in their day-to-day teaching. Kennedy

(1999) referred to the challenges faced by prospective teachers when they enter classrooms as "the problem of enactment," emphasizing that teacher education often does not prepare teacher candidates for practical work in classrooms. New teachers theoretically understand what to do but can't always put their knowledge into practice.

Across the globe, policymakers and teacher educators have increasingly turned toward practicing teachers as sources of information for how to design teacher education programs and the content of their courses (e.g., Darling-Hammond et al., 2017). In contrast, a crisis narrative in many parts of the world about the quality of teachers and teacher shortages has gained traction in recent years, leading to the adoption of practices that can be learned quickly and put into practice with fidelity and automaticity. This current iteration of practice raises critical questions about the centrality of the role of practice in the preparation of teachers and the dangers of divorcing practice from theory and research. It also raises questions about teacher autonomy and the lack of respect for teacher knowledge.

This chapter begins by surveying definitions of practice-based teacher education that span these understandings of practice. We then provide a brief history of the role of practice in teacher education from the seventeenth century to the present. Finally, we turn to the role of practice in the design of three teacher education programs that were initiated in response to perceived crises in teacher education, raising questions about their use of what we consider impoverished notions of practice.

Definitions of Practice-Based Teacher Education

Scholars use a variety of terms for the phenomenon of centering practice in teacher education. The most common term in the United States, and increasingly around the world, is practice-based teacher education (PBTE). While PBTE takes many forms, its emphasis is that practice—rather than theory—is essential for learning to teach. The label "school-based training" is more commonly used in the UK (e.g., Beauchamp et al., 2013); this movement is what Furlong and Lawn (2011) refer to as a "turn to the practical." School-based training indicates the location of initial teacher education as outside of the university and in schools. In the Netherlands, Korthagen and his colleagues use the term "realistic" teacher education to indicate the centrality of student teachers' experiences in the design of teacher education curriculum (Korthagen et al., 2001). Each of these movements emphasize the practical aspects of learning to teach gleaned from observations of classroom teachers. Programs that focus on practice often vary in terms of what they emphasize such as where learning to teach occurs, the length of time spent in schools, the content of courses, and the identification of instructors (e.g., research-informed university professors or practice-informed teachers).

In many parts of the world, teacher education programs establish close relationships with schools that serve as practicum sites. For instance, there are teacher training schools in Finland (Niemi and Jakku-Sihvonen, 2006), professional development schools in the United States (Holmes Group, 1990), university schools in Norway (Lund and Eriksen, 2016), and hub schools in Scotland (Hammerness et al., 2020; Menter and Hulme, 2011). In the United States and the UK, there are residency programs that have varied relationships with schools and districts (e.g., Gatti, 2019; Solomon, 2009). In one common model of teacher residency programs, prospective teachers spend a significant amount of time learning to teach from practicing teachers at the school site, gradually taking on more responsibility for classroom teaching over time. Similarly, there are apprenticeship models in the UK (e.g., Furlong and Lawn, 2011; Steadman, 2018). These programs often focus on preparing teachers for local contexts (Gist et al., 2019). In addition, some programs use community-based settings as sites for learning to teach (Zeichner, 2023).

Rather than using school classrooms as the only site for learning to teach, teacher educators bring practice into the university classrooms, sometimes called "laboratories" for clinical teacher education (Berliner, 1975; Grossman, 2005) and through micro teaching, rehearsals, or practice teaching small groups of peers (e.g., Grossman, 2005; Lampert, 2010; Lampert et al., 2013). Teacher educators have conceptualized this process in very different ways, ranging from intentional and scaffolded practice to modeling and repetition until mastery. In the first instance, student teachers try a practice once and then repeat it for their peers after they receive feedback in order to gain expertise and confidence. Alternatively, teacher educators ask their students to repeat a prescribed teaching move until they achieve automaticity, without opportunities to adapt the practice to particular students and contexts.

In some cases, practice-based teacher education has extended beyond the university or school, as teacher educators turn to virtual sites for learning through the use of simulations and avatars (e.g., Cohen et al., 2020; Kim, 2024). SimSchool is an online platform that claims that prospective teachers can practice teaching students with any type of learning profile they might find in the classroom. While critics worry that the interactions between teachers and students through avatars do not take into account the social and relational aspects of learning to teach (Steadman, 2018), proponents claim that prospective teachers can rehearse teaching moves without putting actual students at risk. (For a review of these studies, see Lindberg and Jönsson, 2023.)

Practice-based teacher education programs sometimes increase the amount of time prospective teachers spend in schools through lengthening practicums or increasing the number of placements or schools where student teachers observe and engage in practice teaching (e.g., Anderson and Stillman, 2012; Forzani, 2014; OECD, 2019). The amount of time in the field can vary from a few weeks to a full year.

In addition to anchoring teacher education to particular locations and specifying the amount of time in clinical settings, increasingly, practice-based teacher education refers to the coursework and pedagogical practices of programs that are developed from practice. Growing out of a desire to center practice in teacher education, scholars have developed the notion of core or high leverage practices. This includes practices that form the architecture of individual courses, as well as the organization of coursework in programs (Ball and Forzani, 2009; Davis and Boerst, 2014; Grossman and Fraefel, 2024; Grossman and McDonald, 2008; Jenset et al., 2018). As Ball and Forzani (2009, p. 503; emphasis ours) explain, "to make practice the core of the curriculum of teacher education requires a shift from a focus on what teachers *know* to a greater focus on what teachers *do*." This notion is grounded in both research and practice and aims to provide prospective teachers with "adaptive expertise" (Janssen et al., 2015) or the ability to apply knowledge and judgement to teaching moments. Similarly, around the world, programs have adopted practices introduced by Lemov (2010) in his popular book, *Teach Like a Champion*, which emphasizes easy-to-learn strategies to manage classrooms and learning, especially in "challenging" urban contexts. Lemov (2013, p. 52) explains that he uses practice in a limited sense: "Practice is a time when colleagues meet together and participate in exercises that encode core skills." While Lemov's set of strategies and the core practice movement are often conflated, their roots are distinct. Nonetheless, all of these choices constitute what various people consider to be practice-based teacher education.

A Brief History of the Role of Practice in Teacher Education

We next turn to the history of practice-based teacher education. In 2010, a US blue-ribbon panel proclaimed that teacher education must be "turned upside down" so that practice is the basis for learning to teach (NCATE, 2010). The election of the Conservative-led coalition government that same year promoted "practice" and the application of teaching "skills" in learning to teach in the UK. Several countries around the world have followed suit (e.g., Darling-Hammond et al., 2017; Jenset et al., 2018).

The history of how practice-based teacher education has become a dominant method for preparing teachers around the world illuminates how the role of practice has been conceptualized in learning to teach. There are several reasons that tracing this history is important. First, there are parallels between early attempts to emphasize practice in learning to teach and today. For instance, in several different time periods, people have attempted to identify which practices should be taught, with the number of these practices ranging from about 20 to over 1,000. In most cases, researchers identified practices through observing teachers in classrooms. A consequence of delineating practices is that too often mandated practices restrict teacher autonomy and supplant teacher judgment. The grain size of practices varies substantially. For instance, practice might encompass teaching more broadly, such as taking an inquiry stance (e.g., Cochran-Smith and Lytle, 2019), or it may be a prescribed action such as using a "strong voice" (Lemov, 2021). Finally, a historical analysis reflects the push and pull between an emphasis on theory taught primarily in the university and practice learned primarily in classrooms, though this tension has shifted over time as practice has been conceptualized as including research and theory and as taught in universities. The various models highlight the decisions that programs make and their reasons for choosing what to emphasize.

Reid (2011) traces the idea of practice as central to learning to teach to the seventeenth century, when de la Salle established the Christian Brothers Schools, initially in France, to train lay teachers to teach children living in poverty. These schools became the model for Normal Schools (post-secondary schools devoted to teacher preparation) that still exist today around the world, where prospective teachers learned to teach through observations in model classrooms and the demonstration of "good" teaching practices by experienced teachers.

Throughout the nineteenth century in the United States and much of the world, the general public's assumption was that teachers did not require specialized training or knowledge, because teaching consisted mostly of lecturing, monitoring students' assignments, and group recitations (Forzani, 2014). Forzani (2014) explains that at the end of the 1800s in the United States, teachers learned to teach in Normal Schools by initially learning skills and then through practice, specific and direct feedback, and, in some cases, a performance exam, similar to the routines adopted by many teacher education programs today around the world. When Normal Schools were transformed into education departments located in colleges and universities, they became more research focused and shifted away from an emphasis on practice-based teacher education. In England and Wales, however, teacher preparation continued to take place in colleges (similar to Normal Schools) rather than universities and practice-based knowledge remained central to the curriculum (Furlong, 2023).

Practice had a lesser role in learning to teach in the United States until the 1920s when the Commonwealth Teacher Training Study attempted to identify all of the activities performed by teachers so that teacher educators could identify the knowledge that was relevant for these activities (Hauser and Kavanagh, 2019; Kennedy, 2016; Zeichner, 2012). A team of researchers asked teachers to list all of their activities and then asked school administrators to look at the lists and identify those they thought were most important for teachers to enact. The result was a list of 1,001 items in seven categories that included activities such as giving students assignments in a range of subject areas. While the purpose was to provide teacher educators with the information they needed to develop a curriculum of "relevant knowledge," as Kennedy (2016) explains, the items were often either too narrow or overly broad. The authors of the study aimed to identify nearly every move a teacher might make in the classroom and teachers were expected to adapt the list of activities to their settings and grade levels. In contrast to contemporary efforts to identify core practices of teaching that are limited in number, the Commonwealth Study was focused primarily on comprehensiveness and detail rather than a unified conception or theory of teaching. The Commonwealth Study, however, had a relatively limited impact on teaching in the United States.

Responding to the dominant educational research of the time, there was a focus on teaching behaviors in the 1960s and 1970s (e.g., Baral et al., 1968 in Forzani, 2014). Led by Lee Shulman (e.g., 1986, 1987), the direction of teacher education in the 1980s moved away from an emphasis on the identification and learning of individual practices toward a focus on the knowledge teachers need in learning to teach.

The most recent turn toward an emphasis on practice coincided with the election of conservative governments in both the UK and United States in the early 2000s. In the UK, beginning in the 1990s, the national conversation about teacher education emphasized the importance of practice, as well as school-based teacher education (Steadman, 2018). While there were concerns about what is lost in the emphasis on practice, there were also many people in support of this focus. In a blog, Fletcher-Wood, Associate Dean at the Institute for Teaching in London, described this position: "Teachers can discuss student learning until the cows come home, with insight and erudition, but it's a waste of time unless they practice behaving differently in the classroom: insight without action is indulgence … . All teacher training should be practise-based" (Fletcher-Wood, 2017 cited in Steadman, 2018).

At about the same time, a movement to define and emphasize core or high leverage practices grew in prominence in the United States. Scholars recognized a need for a common vocabulary to define practice in order to prepare teachers (Bertram and Ruszynak, 2024; Grossman and McDonald, 2008; for a critique of this move toward a common professional language, see Horn and Kane, 2019), which led to the identification of a set of central or core practices. As Forzani (2014) explains, a focus on core practices is more concerned with what and how prospective teachers learn practices, than where the teacher preparation takes place. A curriculum based on core practices is generally focused on complex practices, such as leading discussions, that are described in detail and broken into components. After viewing videos or other records of practice, prospective teachers engage in scaffolded activities to practice in simulated settings with their peers and later in classrooms, where they are often closely coached (e.g., Forzani, 2014; Grossman and McDonald, 2008; Lampert et al., 2013; McDonald et al., 2013). During each of these phases of practice or rehearsal, there is an emphasis on skills such as listening, improvisation, and guiding instructional discourse (Forzani, 2014).

Current Directions in Teacher Education Programs

Several scholars have raised concerns about the core practice movement, which has gained traction across the globe. Steadman (2018) warned that the danger of repetitive practice or rehearsals is that teachers don't gain an understanding of how to adapt their learning to new settings and instead become "expert technicians." She states:

> There is a need, therefore, to explore new and innovative models of teacher education that recognise the transformative nature of teaching and embrace an expansive notion of practice that acknowledges the centrality of social relationships, the individuality of the learning process and the ongoing nature of learning. In the making of teachers, the focus should be on the practice of educating professionals rather than the training of practitioners. (p. 7)

Steadman (2018) argues further that the act of learning to teach is shaped by the teacher. As student teachers begin teaching, their understanding of practice is continuously "reworked and reinvented" (Britzman, 2003, p. 73). Ellis (2010, p. 112) states this point slightly differently: "school-based teacher education also needs to recognise and plan for the agency of beginning teachers in engaging with the social systems within which they are working." Further, several scholars explain that teaching and learning are grounded in relationships and power such that teaching looks different in each context and in each moment it is practiced (Daniels and Varghese, 2019; Dutro and Cartun, 2016). Lampert's (2010) distinction is helpful here: practice can refer to both what the individual does (a teacher's practice) and also to a collective set of practices or tools learned through participation in the practice, and importantly in relationship to people, texts, and places. In other words, Lampert makes the distinction between whether the focus is on teachers learning from another more experienced teacher's practice or on learning a more global set of practices.

Steadman's transformative vision of teacher education has been echoed by several scholars (e.g., Anderson, 2019; Kretchmar and Zeichner, 2016; Philip et al., 2019; Souto-Manning and Martell, 2019) and suggests a new direction for teacher education. She describes the complexity of learning to teach:

> In the making of the teacher, there is no endpoint of perfection at the end of a linear pathway or on completion of an apprenticeship. The practice of learning to teach is an uneven and incomplete process, "practice does not make perfect; practice makes practice" (Hinchion & Hall, 2015, p. 421). But practice is also personal and impossible to define within a set of core practices or instructional tips that can be applied by every teacher in any context.
>
> (Steadman, 2018, p. 6)

A transformative vision of learning to teach that embraces teachers' autonomy, a respect for their judgment, and the upholding of their dignity stands in contrast to a current movement in teacher education that has been fueled by philanthropists in response to critiques of education around the globe.

Three Responses to the "Crisis" in Teacher Education

In this final section, we turn to three examples of graduate programs that center teaching practices that can be learned quickly and put into practice with fidelity and automaticity. Each was developed in response to perceived crises in teaching and teacher education and the need to accelerate the preparation process. The programs present an impoverished view of teachers and teaching, undermining teacher autonomy, degrading teaching as a profession, and eclipsing the possibilities for deep student engagement and learning.

We begin with independent graduate schools of education in the United States, which are independent from universities and often affiliated with charter schools or autonomous public schools and rely on both public and private funding. Next we look at an example of an independent graduate school in the UK that was developed from the US model. Finally, we examine a teacher residency program in the United States, which is a partnership between a university and a private nonprofit created by venture philanthropists. Each of these programs is a response to a crisis narrative that claims that university-based teacher education is too far removed from classroom practice, unyielding in its commitment to theory and research, too lengthy, and essentially broken. The imagined solution is simple: disruption, privatization, and a call for nimble programs freed from the shackles of university-based teacher education (Cochran-Smith et al., 2020; Ellis et al., 2024).

Begun in the early 2000s in the United States, independent graduate schools were primarily established to prepare teachers for specific charter schools and to partner with Teach for America (TFA) so that teachers could meet the minimal state certification requirements. Because of their independence, though they are authorized by states, they are often able to avoid many of the state regulations that govern university-based teacher education programs. As a result, their programs tend to be shorter, staffed by practitioners—often from their affiliated charter schools—and practice based, albeit a more shallow version of practice than many scholars of PBTE advocate (e.g., Kretchmar and Zeichner, 2016).

While these programs vary greatly (e.g., Cochran-Smith, 2020; Cochran-Smith et al., 2020; Cochran-Smith et al., 2022), the guiding principle of most of these programs is that they prepare teachers whose students perform well on high-stakes standardized assessments. In other words, rather than a focus on teacher quality or preparing teachers who remain in teaching, their focus is on short-term gains on standardized tests, as testing is seen as the sole metric for measuring student success and teacher quality. Although independent graduate schools garner both public and private funding, they have represented a key space for philanthropic and venture capital funders to participate in changing—and often privatizing—public education (e.g., Anderson, 2019; Philip et al., 2019).

New York City is an interesting site in the United States to explore the range of teacher preparation programs because of the number of alternative and university-based teacher education programs that exist side by side. The alternative programs were developed as an emergency response to the perceived teacher shortages and concerns about teacher quality, as well as critiques of university-based teacher education that were prevalent in the early 2000s in both the United States and the UK. Many of the alternative programs were funded by both the philanthropic community and federal grants, as funders turned away from the university as the site of teacher education (Zeichner and Peña-Sandoval, 2015). In 2012, TFA, which had initially partnered with university-based programs in New York City, turned to an independent graduate school, Relay Graduate School of Education, for its coursework. Mungal (2016) writes that both TFA and Relay were seen as a "means of privatization of a public good by creating an enterprise for external people to make money" (Mungal, 2012, p. 15 in Mungal 2016). The New Schools Venture Fund (NSVF) played an important role in funding and promoting both a set of independent graduate schools, like Relay, and the "no excuses" charter schools connected to them. Former NSVF CEO Stacy Childress (2016, p. 26) boldly stated, "Teacher preparation is shaping up to be the next frontier for entrepreneurs."

The Relay Graduate School, a program closely connected to three charter networks—Uncommon Schools, the Knowledge Is Power Program (KIPP), and Achievement First—and privately funded by several philanthropies, is the largest independent graduate school in the United States and illustrates an embrace of the notion of disrupting university-affiliated teacher education programs. Initially opened in New York City and now with campuses across the United States, Relay organizes its coursework around Lemov's (2010) forty-nine techniques to become a "champion" teacher in an effort to prepare its students to quickly enter the charter schools affiliated with the program. The leaders at Relay describe their program as a "breakthrough approach" that "emphasises the practical, not the theoretical" and focuses on techniques that will "work on Monday morning" (Relay Graduate School of Education, 2014, in Kretchmar and Zeichner, 2016, p. 423).

Entrepreneurs who poured money into new independent graduate schools borrowed the language of disruption from technology companies to characterize their response to the perceived crisis. Central to the work supported by entrepreneurs is a belief that using best practices as the focus of teacher preparation will lead to the desired outcome of higher scores on standardized assessments (Zeichner and Peña-Sandoval, 2015). In conjunction with fast-track programs such as Teach for America, independent graduate programs are seen as a way to lower barriers and speed up the process of learning to teach by leaning on best practices—that are rapidly learned and practiced for automaticity, standardization, and fidelity—as a solution to the purported crisis in public education.

Located in the UK and founded in 2017, our second example, the Institute for Teaching (IFT), now the Ambition Institute, is an independent graduate school with a wide array of programs for initial teacher education (or in their words, "teacher training"), leadership training, and professional development for teachers and leaders. The attributes of "simplicity, convenience, accessibility, and affordability" dominate the narrative that guides the school (Clayton Christensen Institute for Disruptive Innovation, n.d. in Ellis et al., 2019, p. 105) and mirror the critiques of university-based teacher education in the United States. Not surprisingly, one of the central designers of this program went to the United States to study independent graduate schools, and in particular Relay, for inspiration, returning to the United Kingdom to secure private funding for this endeavor (Ellis et al., 2019; Ellis et al., 2024). The leaders of this initiative defined their programs as "teacher led" (as opposed to led by the university) and practice-focused, using familiar rhetoric to frame the crisis in education and explaining that

> every education system around the world faces two major challenges: closing the stubborn achievement gaps between disadvantaged children and their wealthier peers and ensuring that young people leave compulsory education with the knowledge, skills and characteristics they need in order to thrive in the modern world. Failure to address these challenges is morally indefensible and economically unsustainable.
>
> (Hood, 2016, p. 3 in Ellis et al., 2019)

In addition to addressing the structural challenges of inequality and social mobility, the IFT claimed that their initial teacher education and professional development programs address what they call "teacher plateauing" or their finding (contradicted in educational research) that teachers tend to plateau in their "effectiveness" at five years. Their solution drew on the ideas of psychologist Ericsson who developed the notion of "deliberate practice" that leads to expertise (e.g., Ericsson, 2008). A central idea of the IFT pedagogy is that teaching is like athletics and that in order to improve teaching, teacher educators should select the important practices, break them into their smallest parts, and instruct teachers to practice them until they are mastered, in the same way that athletes work on drills to improve their performance (Ellis et al., 2019).

The reduction of practices in teacher education to simple ideas that can be learned through repetitive practice is appealing to educational entrepreneurs and governmental policymakers who seek solutions to complex problems. It represents the dangers and also the opportunities of the current time, which we elaborate in the next chapter.

A third example is an urban teacher residency program in the United States, that is a partnership between a private nonprofit created by venture philanthropists, Leaders for Equity in Education, and a university (Gatti, 2019; Gatti and Catalano, 2015). Teacher residency programs were developed in part to address persistent teacher shortages and formed through collaborative relationships between districts and universities. Teachers are paid and given a stipend in their first year with the expectation that they will commit to teaching for the next three or four years in that same district (cf., National Academy of Education, 2024; Solomon, 2009).

In the residency program documented by Gatti and Catalano (2015; Gatti, 2019), prospective teachers took an initial course in the summer based on the strategies promoted by Lemov (2010). In an explanation reminiscent of the logic of the IFT program, the teacher profiled by Gatti and Catalano (2015, p. 154) explains:

> But that's also part of the Lemov, every minute counts because we're closing the achievement gap we have to be careful how we use each minute. Minutes spent dealing with somebody for disciplinary or whatever is a minute not spent on instruction and closing the achievement gap. That's one of the strategies. Every minute counts.

As Gatti (2019) summarizes, the primary goal of the Lemov material and this residency program is to teach techniques that are "specific, concrete, and actionable" and which provide a "tool box for closing the achievement gap" (p. 3).

In addition to the Lemov strategies, this program uses a process whereby teachers become what Gatti and Catalano (2015) call a "remote control teacher." The program uses "real time coaching," which means that at any point during their classroom teaching, the mentor teacher can stop the action in order to model for the resident how they should teach. In addition, at any time, supervisors, coaches, administrators, or other residents are encouraged to come into their classrooms to either watch or videotape their teaching. As a result, teachers are "trained" and then monitored (and in some cases, tested) in their performance of practices with fidelity.

Lemov, Woolway, and Yezzi (2012) explain the reasoning behind the strategies:

> Once you have learned a skill to automaticity, your body executes, and only afterwards does your mind catch up … [you] do it without thinking and this is exactly the point … . The takeaway: You don't have to be aware of your knowledge to use it. In fact, awareness often gets in the way. (pp. 33–6)

The close monitoring of prospective teachers to ensure compliance and fidelity allows teachers to attain automaticity while severely limiting their autonomy. We worry about what happens when practice becomes so narrowly defined. In many ways, some of the current uses of practices in teacher preparation, particularly in many of the independent graduate schools of education, recall ideas from the 1970s or even earlier, rather than reflecting current scholarship on learning to teach, including the importance of humanizing and culturally sustaining pedagogies (Paris and Alim, 2017; Paris and Winn, 2013). In addition, the erosion of teacher autonomy, as exemplified by these teacher education programs, means that teaching is no longer a vibrant and creative activity that people choose as a long-term career. Instead teaching becomes rote and more about compliance than a commitment to the public good.

Conclusion: Beyond Social Justice and Towards Expansive Notions of Practice

In her reflections on the relationship between theory and practice, Keffrelyn Brown (2013) powerfully articulates the dangers of relying on shallow versions of practice in place of wrestling with issues of race and racist discourses that shape teaching and learning. She worries about the dangers of adopting a single method for teaching all children.

> While I recognize the importance that learning how to enact practice plays in learning to teach, I would also argue that viewing theory and practice as disconnected elements creates the conditions where pre-service teachers ultimately fail to engage in and take seriously the intellectual and reflective work needed to understand how racist discourses inform all aspects of the teaching and learning process. It also places an inordinate focus on identifying the one method that will ensure success, regardless of the specific time and space contexts that operate in the teaching environment. This particular gap in knowledge makes it possible for school districts and teachers to seek instructional materials designed to improve the school experiences of students of color and those from low-income backgrounds, but that themselves, rest on racist, classist, monolithic and deficit-oriented approaches to teaching (e.g. see Payne 2005[1996]). It also sends an implied message that only certain types of curriculum, pedagogy and classroom designs – i.e. often those that are prescriptive, directive and rote (Haberman, 1991) are useful for black students.
>
> (Brown, 2013, pp. 328–9)

Several Black scholars powerfully provide the conceptual understanding Brown calls for. In his social history of Black educators who learned to teach through powerful teacher networks, Givens (2021) documents the "fugitive pedagogies" enacted by Black educators. Givens begins his historical account with the story of Tessie McGee, a Black secondary social studies teacher in the 1930s, who taught in the only Black secondary school in Webster, Louisiana. He describes how in McGee's classroom, students would often sit with textbooks on their desks, while she would place the state-mandated and approved outline on her own desk. McGee would read aloud passages from Carter G. Woodson's history of Blacks in America to the students, switching to the mandated text when the principal entered her classroom and taking an enormous risk in order to educate her students. Drawing on the work of Best and Hartman (2005, p. 4), Givens explains his use of the term "fugitive":

> When it came to the pursuit of freedom through education, black people consistently deployed fugitive tactics. Enslaved people learned in secret places. During Jim Crow, black educators wore a mask of compliance in order to appease the white power structure, while simultaneously working to subvert it.

He elaborates how teachers, like McGee, risked their jobs, and perhaps their lives, to teach about not only the instances of degradation that they had experienced, but also the achievements of Black Americans missing from their texts. As Givens (2021, p. 4) states, "an amassed set of values and traditions, I am arguing, stood at the core of the covert demeanors and tool kit of practices necessary to advance the plot of black education."

In his book, *Learning While Black and Queer*, Brockenbrough (2024) uses the framework of fugitivity to uncover and understand how schools and other educational spaces are sites of trans suffering or the multiple and intersecting oppressions that trans youth experience. Rather than equating contemporary Black suffering with the experience of enslaved people, he explains that contemporary scholars use fugitivity to

> trace slavery's indelible imprint on the American experience to explore the ever-present shadow of Black containment,

> the precarity of Black humanity, and the resultant strategies for Black survival and resistance, all of which mirror the remnant contours of an enslaved past.
>
> (Brockenbrough, 2024, p. 71)

One of the questions Brockenbrough (2024) asks is, what are the practices that Black students must develop to survive anti-Black schooling contexts? In this question and his analysis, Brockenbrough moves the focus from teachers' pedagogical practices to those taken up by students, arguing for an examination of students' fugitive practices to inform educators. For instance, he explains that by taking a fugitive perspective, educators can observe the vulnerability and marginalization of students who experience domination or oppression by their peers. Urging educators to uncover and make violence visible as they build and support fugitive spaces, he points to specific kinds of support that the marginalized youth sought and found in the queer-youth-focused community center he studied.

Bettina Love (2019) writes powerfully about abolitionist teaching that has parallels to fugitive pedagogy and stands in stark contrast to the direction that many teacher education programs, and particularly independent graduate schools, have gone in their adoption of practice-based teacher education. Her definition of abolitionist teaching as "choosing to engage in the struggle for educational justice knowing that you have the ability and human right to refuse oppression and refuse to oppress others, mainly your students" (2019, p. 2) mirrors Brockenbrough's focus on addressing oppression. She explains that abolitionist teaching is not a series of strategies nor is it a pedagogical approach; it involves seeing the world through the lens of justice and taking action. She concludes that the ultimate goal of abolitionist teaching is freedom. Love continues: "Abolitionist teaching is the practice of working in solidarity with communities of color while drawing on the imagination, creativity, refusal, (re)membering, visionary thinking, healing, rebellious spirit, boldness, determination, and subversiveness of abolitionists to eradicate injustice in and outside of schools" (p. 2).

Each of these scholars provides a counterpoint to the narrow understandings of practice that have been so readily adopted by teacher education programs around the world. As we have advocated throughout this book, teaching inherently involves a robust, evolving definition of teacher practice that centers relationships. We contend that it is essential to examine the role of practice in learning to teach through history and a range of perspectives. This entails going beyond bringing together practice-based teacher education and social justice education, as many scholars have skillfully done (e.g., Calabrese Barton et al., 2020; Kavanagh and Danielson, 2020; Schierra, 2021; Souto-Manning, 2019) to reimagining teaching through lenses such as fugitive pedagogy and abolitionist teaching in order to examine the discourses and epistemologies of learning to teach that remain unexamined (Varghese et al., 2019). In the next chapter, we explore how the discourses of marketization and privatization have shaped educational practices at a systemic level.

CHAPTER 3

Marketization, Privatization, and Impoverished Notions of Practice

As we look across the ways practice is used in relation to teachers' work, the idea of "best practices" comes up time and time again. The idea of best practices originated in the business world but quickly made its way into educational circles. This idea provides clear justification for why practice is so important as a keyword in teacher education. While, at first glance, it is hard to argue with the logic of employing best practices—who wouldn't want the best implemented in classrooms—further interrogation shows the ways that best practices are often tied to larger political projects and, ultimately, to marketization and privatization efforts. In this chapter, we demonstrate that a robust exploration of practice brings into focus the way these efforts are undermining both economic and democratic purposes of education. A lens of practice helps us to see the ways that prioritizing profits and scalability in educational models limits the scope and autonomy of teachers' work, and ultimately shifts the definition of what it means to be a teacher in ways that do not align with robust student learning and growth.

The conversation around marketization and privatization in education is generally carried out in dense academic language, filled with jargon, and accessible only to other academics. We participate in these conversations, and in no sense mean to undermine their import and value, but we also wonder about the ways that the people whose day-to-day lives are most affected by rampant privatization and marketization—in this case, teachers—are not connected to these conversations. Teachers and students most directly feel the inequities of marketization policies. If we aim to create regulatory environments that support all students, and challenge policies that undermine equity, teachers must have an understanding of and a voice in these conversations.

Teacher educators can support students and practicing teachers in these efforts. Educators should be aware of the ways that marketization and privatization efforts are shaping educational circumstances in their local contexts. We argue that teachers and teacher educators bring important perspectives to this conversation that all of us could learn from. As in our other chapters, an interrogation of practice brings these ideas into relief. Here, we focus particularly on best practices, and the way the discourse of best practices operates to shape educational policy and support marketization efforts.

Definitions of Marketization and Privatization in Education

Part of the issue with discussing and seeking to understand marketization and privatization efforts in education is that many people who do not directly research these trends don't have clarity about their definitions and significance. We turn to a discussion in this vein, meant to clarify understandings of these terms.

In educational scholarship, the terms marketization and privatization are often used interchangeably; there is good reason for this, as the two trends are related at the policy level and are often motivated by similar political agendas (Hogan and Thompson, 2017; Lubienski, 2006; Zancajo et al., 2025). It can be useful, though, to understand the difference since it can help us to better understand the effects these trends have on educational systems (Lubienski and Malin, 2025).

Privatization "can be defined as a process through which private organizations and individuals participate increasingly and actively in a range of education activities and responsibilities that traditionally have been the remit of the state" (Verger et al., 2016, p. 5). In the case of schools, private organizations like corporations or NGOs control aspects of schooling that would usually be controlled by local and state governments. It is important to note that in education, privatization looks different than it does in other parts of the public sector. Usually, when we think of privatizing, we imagine that ownership changes. For example, when public utilities privatize, a private company owns the utilities that were previously publicly owned. In education, though, ownership does not usually change with privatization. The state maintains ownership of schools, but outsources services, often forming public–private partnerships (or PPPs). This is important because when we talk about privatization, we usually imagine the state retreating or becoming smaller; we imagine limitations on government involvement. In contrast, when education privatizes, government involvement is not limited, but redefined, and sometimes even expanded (Jabbar, 2016; Ganti, 2014). Instead of providing all educational services, governments instead shift to a more regulatory role. For example, rather than mandating a structured curriculum, or providing transportation and school lunch, the government is more likely to monitor and evaluate school performance. An important component of privatization is that it creates a need for new regulatory frameworks and policies that support investors' goals of generating profit (Greer and Doellgast, 2017). As illustrated in the New Orleans example discussed later in this chapter, it can concentrate power differently, in this case shifting control from the local government to the state.

Scholars agree that privatization is expanding rapidly on a global scale, especially in recent years; it is a major trend driving educational change worldwide. This is true across an exceptionally wide range of countries despite significant differences in cultural, political, and economic contexts (Verger et al., 2016). Shifts toward privatization are especially pronounced in the global south, particularly with the rise of low-fee private schools (LFPSs) (Bennell, 2024), as we discuss later in this chapter. Different countries follow different pathways to privatizing. For a substantive review of pathways toward privatization across national contexts, see Verger et al., 2017.

Privatization efforts garner both widespread support and significant opposition. Supporters of privatization imagine that it will expand choice, improve quality, and increase equity. While privatization is sometimes painted as a conservative movement, the truth is that diverse coalitions support privatization. Interestingly, the parties may have strikingly divergent interests and beliefs—liberal parent advocacy groups and conservative think tanks, for example—but come together around shared beliefs in the market. Ball (2007) effectively challenges the blanket arguments against privatization. He argues that there is no going back to a time before privatization. Further, he points out that trying to return to a public sector that worked equitably to support the interests of all learners is a fantasy, since this never really existed. On a more philosophical level, Lubienski and Malin (2025) point to the way that tensions between public and private conceptions of education existed long before modern debates about privatization; people seek individual benefit from education, even as the wider community benefits from its availability.

Marketization and privatization are deeply intertwined, although distinct processes. When we talk about the marketization of education, we are referring to the injection of market principles, like school choice, deregulation, and competition, into the public school sector (Bartlett et al., 2002). The concept of marketization helps us to understand a wide range of activities "including the move to non-state providers, contracting out, per-pupil funding schemes, public–private partnerships, testing and accountability policies, and performance-based funding" (Lubienski and Malin, 2025, p. 32). The arguments of market-based reformers are familiar to most of us by now. Broadly, the idea is that competition will provide students with better educational opportunities by making schools more efficient and encouraging innovation. While marketized reform is often framed as increasing equity, it tends to create new inequalities and exacerbate existing ones (Sahlberg, 2023; Zancajo et al., 2025).

Lubienski and Malin (2025) argue for a conceptual distinction between privatization and marketization, pointing out that both supporters and detractors use these terms in ways that are imprecise and obscure the broader processes they refer to. They point out that opposition to privatization is often better characterized as opposition to marketization; in other words, people oppose the "introduction of market roles and mechanisms such as consumer and competition into the public sector" (p. 33). While the reasons used to justify marketization are often similar to the reasons for privatization (e.g., increase efficiency, support greater equity), no entity needs to be privatized for marketization processes to unfold. Zancajo et al. (2025) suggest that in many ways the notion of marketization is a more useful analytic than the notion of privatization, as it helps to comprehensively explain what happens when individual interests are centered in education.

A third word that comes up in conversation with marketization and privatization is neoliberalism. Like marketization, the word neoliberalism is regularly used in conversations about education, but it is often poorly defined or misunderstood. Brown argues that neoliberalism is best understood as a governing rationality that disseminates market values and metrics into every sphere of life (Brown, 2015). Reed (2006) expands on this, arguing that neoliberalism aims to change mindsets, naturalizing ideas that private is always better than public and that the main function of government is to enhance opportunities for the investor class and suppress wages for everyone else. In other words, we come to understand our jobs, our interactions, even ourselves in terms of the market and—perhaps most importantly—this feels natural to us.

Often, people talk about neoliberal mindsets or frameworks driving privatization and marketization trends. While there is truth in this, it is important to note that neoliberalism is not the only driver of educational marketization and privatization; some of the driving forces for these trends exist outside even the broadest definitions of the term. That said, the broad adoption of market values into everyday life fundamentally reshapes our thinking, even for those of us who may try to resist this trend (Jones and Ball, 2023). Perhaps the reason these values have taken hold so strongly in the educational sphere is because many of the processes and practices associated with education fit naturally with this sort of mindset. It just makes sense to try to improve test scores and increase teacher effectiveness in achieving these scores. This is a logic that is hard to argue with and hard to break out of. The neoliberal mindset makes it much harder to ask why we are giving the test, or what it means for a teacher to be effective in the first place. Further complicating the matter, it is dishonest to simply argue wholesale against market values; efficiency at a task and thinking about learning as measurable growth, for example, are not inherently bad ideas, either from a moral perspective or when considering the best interests of teachers and students. What becomes concerning is when these ideas merge with goals of profitability and scalability, at the expense of student learning.

Scholars and journalists frequently write about what the broad global trends toward marketization and privatization mean for public education around the world. But what does all of this have to do with practice? A key argument we aim to make in this chapter is that the discourse of best practices, along with a general disregard for the complexity of teachers' work and teacher autonomy, allows for the exportation of global models of teaching and learning without sufficient attention to history or context. Marketization efforts, in particular, can often only proceed if teachers are imagined as disposable and the complexity of teachers' practice is disregarded. We turn now to two examples to illustrate this point.

Marketization, Privatization, and Impoverished Notions of Practice

LFPSs and Their Proliferation in the Global South

Low-fee private schools (LFPSs) provide perhaps the most striking window into the global educational industry and the way discourses of best practices fuel and support its growth. LFPSs target low-income students and their families, promising social mobility. These schools started to take hold around 2010 in Africa and continue to boom in India and across the African continent. In these contexts, LFPSs set themselves apart from the troubled public school system by drawing on the same language deployed by elite private schools attended by the upper classes, particularly discourses around internationalism and the intensive application of technology (Kagan and Gez, 2021). They enter our conversation because of their views on teacher training, and their reliance on best practices as a way to quickly train and support teachers. These schools explicitly support best practices as a way to de-professionalize teachers, suggesting that if best practices are laid out in a simple manner then anyone can follow them; teachers simply need to perform the curriculum (rather than actually teach).

The example we focus on here is Bridge International Academies (BIA), one of the most prominent providers in the LFPS sector. The first Bridge Academy opened in 2009 in Nairobi, Kenya. Since then, they have expanded operations across Africa and India, garnering financial support from a wide range of philanthropists and organizations including Bill Gates, Mark Zuckerberg, and the World Bank (Riep, 2019b). As BIA grew, they estimated that by 2022, they would educate 4.1 million students and generate $470 million in revenue (Tyre, 2017). In recent years, though, they have struggled in their efforts to scale their operations. The organization has been met with protests and failures preventing them from reaching their expansion goals. Despite this, BIA continues to rebrand and seek ways to make a profit in the global education market (Riep, 2019a).

BIA schools rely on impoverished notions of teachers and teachers' work to make their model financially viable. In other words, these schools are not looking for educated, high-quality teachers; instead, they hire underqualified teachers and pay them wages below the poverty line to reduce operating costs and ensure overall profitability. Philanthropic investments will not sustain the model beyond its initial funding, so the schools have to make a profit to remain in existence. This positions teachers as a primary place for cost cutting, and the discourse of best practices is key to this justification.

BIA's position is that they do not need certified teachers since best practices guide their curriculum. The curriculum and pedagogical instructions for teachers are developed at BIA headquarters in the United States. They are then sent electronically to all school sites via tablet. These so-called teacher computers tell teachers exactly what to do and say throughout the school day. From this perspective, anyone who can read the instructions on the tablet can do the job of a teacher by directly implementing best practices. There is no local input, no adaptation, and no space for teachers to act as professionals and meet the academic and social needs of the students. This impoverished view of practice makes the day-to-day work of teaching difficult, if not impossible, in these schools, even as it helps to ensure their profitability. The discourse of best practices helps to sidestep real engagement with the challenges that emerge on the ground as the model is implemented.

Multiple studies have demonstrated the way the BIA model prioritizes profitability and scalability over the actual provision of a quality education (Härmä, 2017; Riep, 2019b; Riep and Machacek, 2016). BIA schools operate according to an "academy in a box" model; wherever the schools are opened, the practices of teaching and learning are the same (Kirchgasler, 2016), based on the idea of "replication and rapid scalability" (Riep, 2019b). As such, the best practices delivered on teacher computers both undercut teacher autonomy and help support the rapid recruitment of teachers for new schools. Critical, here, is that despite references to best practices, the curriculum is not modeled on peer-reviewed educational research. With profit as the motive, BIA schools are modeled on business principles that are more aligned with successfully running a fast-food chain than a school (Härmä, 2017); the founders of BIA themselves directly compare the successful operation of BIA schools to operating a Starbucks chain (Srivastava, 2016). Capitalizing on parents' desires and fears for their children, these schools use best practices to manage a discursive maneuvering that undermines more viable educational models.

The prioritization of profits and scalability over educational quality has become normalized in conversations about education worldwide; through the lens of practice, we see the problems with this normalization, and we also see a space for resistance, as we reclaim and assert the complexity of teachers' work. We turn now to another example, the charterization of the New Orleans school system after hurricane Katrina, showing once again how impoverished notions of practice pave the way for marketization efforts.

The Charterization of New Orleans in the United States

On August 29, 2005, Hurricane Katrina hit the city of New Orleans, registering as one of the costliest and most destructive natural disasters in recent history. The levees failed and over 80 percent of the city was flooded. More than 1000 people died, and total damage to the region was estimated at $151 billion (Plyer et al., 2015). Post Katrina, New Orleans became both a poster child for and experimentation lab around urban education reform, and market-based educational reforms more specifically, in the United States. New Orleans is regularly cited as the prime example of market-based education reform in the United States (Buras, 2011; Buras, 2016; Jabbar, 2015; Henry and Dixson, 2016) and, interestingly, on the international stage as well (Hook, 2021; Offutt-Cheney, 2022). While we can learn many lessons from what happened to education in New Orleans post Katrina, here we focus specifically on how these reforms affected teachers and teacher practice.

Katrina decimated schools in New Orleans. Eighty percent of the public schools were damaged or destroyed by the storm (Buras, 2015). Prior to Katrina, the Orleans Parish School Board (OPSB) controlled 128 public schools in the city of New Orleans, and had an operating budget of approximately $419 million (Buras, 2013). In the aftermath of the storm, it became possible for the state to take control of the majority of the city's schools from the OPSB. Charter schools emerged as the primary vehicle for rebuilding and reopening schools. In the aftermath of the storm, the state run Recovery School District (RSD) gained control of 107 of the schools, chartering the majority of them (Buras, 2011). By 2015, the district was completely chartered (Jabbar, 2016).

We focus here on two related effects at the classroom level: shifts in the composition of the teacher workforce and shifts in teacher pedagogy and practice across the district. It is important to situate these shifts in the context of the deep ties many district teachers had with their communities and the robust pedagogies that placed community tradition and history at the center of the curriculum prior to the storm. In-depth exploration of jazz, Mardi Gras, the history of these traditions, and their ongoing importance to the Black community, were embedded throughout the curriculum as educators brought their lives and the lives of other community members into the classroom (Buras, 2013; Offut-Cheney, 2022). Prior to the storm, the teachers' notions of practice were complex, centering relationships and community and using this as the foundation for student learning and growth. In contrast, as the marketization of the city's schools proceeded, it relied on shallow understandings of teachers' practice and work. As we saw in the BIA example, the discourse of best practices enabled this, providing cover for the firing of veteran teachers and the impoverished versions of teacher practice that followed.

In late 2005, as the state moved to consolidate control, district teachers were served notice that their positions would be terminated; about 6,000 veteran teachers, the majority of whom were Black, were fired en masse in early 2006. The teachers were fired without due process and without regard for the many rights they had fought for over the past decades. Their pensions were abolished, and they were left without health insurance. Those who remained in the revamped system lost these benefits, as veteran teachers with twenty and thirty years of experience were reclassified as first-year employees with respect to the pension system, and health insurance premiums rose to over $1,000 a month (Buras, 2013; Klein, 2007; Miron, 2008). The composition of the teacher workforce changed dramatically as charterization proceeded. Post Katrina, the teacher workforce in New Orleans became significantly whiter and less experienced overall. For example, in 2004–5, the academic year prior to Katrina, about 75 percent of teachers in New Orleans were Black. By 2010, less than half of teachers across both RDS schools and OPSB schools were Black; further, nearly 40 percent of teachers in New Orleans had less than three years of teaching experience, and white teachers rose from 24 to 46 percent across the city (Buras, 2016).

These shifts could not have happened without government partnership with and support for Teach for America (TFA), along with an impoverished view of practice that disregarded teacher knowledge and experience. Importantly, TFA claims that teachers can be trained quickly and easily by relying on models of best practices. Partnership with TFA is a common theme in US school systems that have shifted toward greater privatization; while this is not explicitly part of the mission of TFA, researchers have pointed to the way that TFA acts as part of a broader nexus of privatization, playing a critical role in making privatization possible (e.g., Kretchmar, 2014). Further, TFA's internal success with diversity efforts—the corps has become increasingly more diverse over time—provided cover for the way the organization often displaces veteran educators of color (White, 2016). If teachers' work is imagined in simplistic terms, if teachers are easy to train and replace, and if organizations like TFA exist to efficiently provide this labor, marketization can proceed.

TFA fit well with the RSD's "no experience necessary" stance for hiring. While we know from research that teachers' practice evolves over time, and healthy school communities have teachers from a range of experience levels, reformers at the state and national level focused on affordability and minimized concerns around experience. Their decisions around hiring were driven primarily by economic concerns. This is perhaps best captured in a quote by Paul Vallas when he was the superintendent of the RSD, praising temporary recruits and nonunionized charters:

> I don't want the majority of my teaching staff to work more than 10 years. The cost of sustaining those individuals becomes so enormous. Between retirement and healthcare and things like that, it means that you are constantly increasing class sizes and cutting programs in order to sustain the cost of a veteran workforce, so I think you want a mix, you want a balance.
>
> (Conway, 2010)

Again, this stance is only possible without a robust understanding of practice. For Vallas, TFA represented not only an opportunity to shift toward a more affordable workforce, but also a chance to more tightly control and define curricular purposes; standardized test scores became central to his evolving accountability regime.

The mass firings in New Orleans were devastating for veteran teachers who were trying to rebuild their lives after the storm. Relatedly, the firings had profound equity implications for students, who were now being taught by teachers with significantly less experience. Some of these implications are well-documented, and mirror the exacerbations of inequity that are commonly associated with privatization. Less talked about is how this shift toward novice and largely untrained teachers within a charter framework shifted teacher practice and thus the conditions for student learning.

This move to inexperienced teachers, supplied largely by TFA, changed the character and composition of classroom practice across New Orleans. Some studies have documented the way that TFA teachers tend to rely on what we call shallow versions of practice (e.g., Brewer, 2014; Crawford-Garrett, 2013; Veltri, 2010). Sondel's (2014, 2015, 2017) qualitative research is especially interesting in this regard. For example, she followed TFA teachers over the course of an academic year at a KIPP school in New Orleans (Sondel, 2015), considering teacher beliefs about the purposes of schooling and the shifts in practice these beliefs entailed. KIPP schools are charter schools that were started by two TFA alumni; over time this network has become quite large and influential. She found that while the teachers were diverse in their goals, and some were genuinely committed to robust understandings of democratic education and social justice, their pedagogical decisions were undercut by the structure of the charter school and the demands of standardized tests. Daily teaching and learning in these classrooms, despite the general orientation of the teacher, focused on gaining student compliance through behavioral rather than communal methods of classroom management and preparing students directly for performance on standardized tests. Further, most teachers left their school within three years, which meant they never had time to develop pedagogies that could both support students on assessments while also cultivating deeper learning and the development of democratic citizenship.

What Do We Learn by Thinking Across These Two Examples?

Sometimes marketization trends are written off as larger policy issues, removed from the day-to-day work of teaching. These two examples remind us how these trends directly shape teachers' work conditions and limit their capacity to act in ways that holistically support student learning and growth. In LFPSs, we see teacher decision making replaced with tablets and a tightly scripted curriculum developed from afar. In New Orleans, we see a network of privatization dramatically shift the teacher workforce and ultimately teaching and learning in classrooms across the city. In both cases, we see how impoverished notions of teachers' practice pave the way for marketization efforts that dramatically redefine the nature of teachers' work. Further, they shape professional contexts in ways that lead many teachers to leave classrooms and others to take on diminished roles. It is useful for new teachers—especially teachers who are teaching in heavily marketized districts—to understand this, and also to look beyond it, seeking out robust models of teacher learning and teacher practice.

In this vein, we ask: What are the commonalities across these cases that help us to build programs that support teachers in evaluating and, when necessary, challenging marketization and privatization efforts in ways that protect their own autonomy and support student learning? As we think across the BIA and New Orleans examples, two specific lessons emerge that can help to inform program design, highlighting the kinds of activism teachers can incorporate into their practice.

Lesson One: We Can Teach Teachers to Analyze, Evaluate, and Resist Accountability Regimes

It is important for teachers to understand that discourses of best practices and accountability regimes are part of a broader ecosystem that drives privatization and creates space for new actors in education. In the LFPS example, we see how NGOs and for-profit organizations step into the space traditionally held by the government and institutes of higher education. In the New Orleans example, we see how organizations like Teach for America are tied to and prop up accountability regimes and ideas of best practices, creating a network that ultimately changes ideas about what it means to be a practicing teacher, prioritizing test performance as the sole measure of educational outcomes. Across both examples, we see how best practices support a vision of teaching and learning that undermines teacher autonomy and narrowly aims to increase test scores.

Teacher education curricula are often too packed and tightly controlled by state regulations to leave room for conversations and learning about the impact of marketization on practice. Accountability regimes and standardized tests have profoundly changed the work of teaching, pushing even the most committed teachers to cater their work to test performance, as they simultaneously try to make time and space for practices that promote deeper learning. Accountability regimes reduce teacher autonomy, and excellent educators leave the classroom because they do not have the space or time to call on their own expertise and intuition to create learning environments that best serve children. It is critical that prospective teachers understand the linkages between these accountability regimes and the broader projects of privatization and marketization, as well as the ties to discourses of best practices, shifts in teacher employment practices, and ultimately shifts in our very ideas of how practice relates to teaching and learning. As teacher educators, the more we understand these ties, and appreciate the interconnected web they form, the more thoughtful we can be about how we create spaces that support teachers in nurturing and preserving complex notions of practice.

As part of the research for this book, we spoke with both scholars who study practice and practicing teachers about their evolving sense of practice. One of the teachers we spoke with, Shaina—an educator who strongly identified her teaching as a form of activism—talked explicitly about her struggle with accountability regimes, even as she made strategic choices to resist them.

> I've also self-selected into non-Regents (New York state test) spaces…which also creates problems … many times students are like, okay, I guess we have to do this project, largely because it is a graduation requirement. And I taught in an elective space that was not a graduation requirement, and I saw how quickly I was losing young people, because at a certain point in the school year, they were like, We are kind of done. We've finished … all of the standardized test-based stuff. And so why do we have to still keep working hard when you know we're not necessarily being rewarded by the system for this work? And so that's also another space of challenge. It's like testing has fundamentally structured young people's relationship to learning and engagement. And so even when things are fun, even when they are self-selected, even when they are meaningful, there's a lot of coaching that has to go into like learning for the sake of learning, engagement for the sake of engagement, not just for the test, not just for a grade, not just to set you up with an internship or a job, which are some of the ways that we've tried to get buy in, and I'm sure that that's a challenge that's just going to keep getting harder.

What can we do as teacher educators to better prepare teachers to meet and engage the kinds of challenges Shaina describes? As a starting point, we can make these concerns around accountability regimes explicit in our pedagogies with new teachers, modeling for them the kinds of struggles they too will face as they encounter austerity measures and seek to advocate for their own professionalism in public schools.

Lesson Two: We Can Teach Teachers That Schooling Decisions Are Political, and That Their Voice Is Critical to These Conversations

A common refrain is that we expect far too much from teachers already, given that they are overworked and underpaid; it isn't fair to also expect them to be activists. While we profoundly agree that teachers should be better compensated and better supported, literature—along with our own experience and connections with practicing educators—suggests that many teachers find activism deeply sustaining. This is true whether teachers enter the classroom believing teaching is a political act, or come to learn this over time, unsatisfied with their own lack of autonomy and ability to practice as they see fit. Anyon (2005) writes about this notion robustly, and Givan and Lang's (2020) edited volume offers a range of perspectives that shows this trend among educators across political lines. When we asked Shaina how she thought we could support teachers in joining theory and practice, she, tellingly, chose to talk about recruitment and calling, arguing that teacher education programs must take a stance themselves:

> I think we are entering an era in this world in which we desperately need teachers who are brave and who are courageous and who are committed to truth-telling and committed to standing up for what's right and committed to protecting their young people. And so maybe it is a matter

> of just being a lot more explicit about like, you know, these are the values of the program, and if you're not with us, you can get a part time master's degree online very easily to be a teacher. That's not what this program is here for. This program is here to build activist educators. That's what the commitments of the program are. And you know, that's who we look for, and that's who we are here to support, because that's who we need right now in our classrooms.

Ultimately, new teachers can learn to see marketization efforts as critical to push back against when they interfere with their day-to-day practices. In our teacher education programs, we can invite teachers to resist educational privatization and marketization not because these processes are inherently bad, but because of the documented ways in which they can build on and further existing inequalities in our educational system. As Fontdevila et al. (2025, p. 478) explain in their recent handbook on privatization and marketization:

> Different country cases demonstrate that the primary driver behind the problematisation of education privatization and marketization is the inequalities they tend to generate. Evidence from various contexts shows that pro-market policies in education tend to widen the achievement gaps between socially disadvantaged and affluent students, and increase school segregation and social stratification between schools. (Macpherson et al., 2014; Waslander et al., 2010; OECD, 2012; Alegre and Ferrer, 2010)

That said, there is no inevitability to the outcomes of market-based interventions; they can feed and further existing inequalities, or, critically, they can also be repurposed to serve the ends of equity (Zancajo et al., 2025). Jabbar (2016) points to the role local governments play in marketization by opening schools, closing schools, making sure schools meet quality standards, and so on. If we support teachers to better understand these regulating functions, they can find ways to intervene in local politics and beyond, pushing to make educational markets more fair and equitable.

As teacher educators, we can do more than rally against privatization and marketization in our own work, or simply teach our students to critique these trends. We can develop curriculum to help them recognize and enter into the politics of school regulation, beginning with what they can change in their own schools and districts. We can work with them to recognize the ways in which they can have a say at the local level and beyond about the kinds of regulatory environments in our schools. We can teach them how critical their perspective is; nothing is more important to these conversations than authentic portraits of day-to-day practice, yet teacher perspectives are often entirely missing. We can help them think about the most effective ways to make their voices heard by holding similar conversations in our own classrooms and supporting new teachers to continue to engage in this work once they leave our programs.

Conclusion: Practice, Collective Action, and Community

By way of conclusion, we turn to examples of practicing teachers who have engaged in activist efforts. One of the ways teachers have resisted the negative effects marketization has on their work is through teacher strikes. While we hope for a future where teachers can claim a seat at the table without needing to resort to collective action, we also note that globally, strikes have been one of the only ways teachers can make their voices heard in the face of austerity measures. Teacher unions have been key actors in resistance to marketization. It's striking to note that we see the inverse of this in the New Orleans example; it was actually the displacement of a powerful union and community residents by a natural disaster that paved the way for the district to prioritize market principles and to charterize. Quite literally, no one was there to object and marketization moved forward.

Globally, teacher strikes often foment or ground broader social movements aimed at resisting the more marginalizing and disempowering impacts of privatization and marketization across social sectors. The teacher strikes in Oaxaca, Mexico, in 2006 are an excellent example of this. Stephen's (2013) thoughtful work chronicles the way that an annual protest by a teacher union in Oaxaca, demanding higher wages and better school funding, ultimately fueled a broader social movement that continues to this day, galvanizing indigenous resistance and grassroots organizing. Similar examples can be seen in other parts of South America, like the recent strikes in Chile and Argentina. In Africa, teachers in Kenya and Zimbabwe have held strikes to demand better pay and resist austerity measures, and in Nigeria, teachers have pushed back against disrespect for teacher labor, as teacher unions are undermined and "volunteer teachers" who lack job security and benefits replace union teachers. In the United States, the Red for Ed movement, along with strikes in more democratic strongholds like Chicago and Los Angeles, have followed a similar pattern. Across these examples, we see teachers acting to defend education as a public good, often collaborating with unions across the public sector to resist austerity measures and push back against marketization.

While strikes provide one way teachers can make their voices heard, we also emphasize here what undergirds these efforts, and is at the heart of many veteran teachers' work: the value of teacher community and collective learning. In past years, as a way to conclude an introductory teacher education course, we have asked seasoned educators from two teacher collaboratives in New York City—MORE (Movement of Rank and File Educators) and NYCORE (New York Collective of Radical Educators)—to come to class and participate on a panel. These educators discuss with prospective teachers how they stay hopeful and engaged as they work in some of the city's most challenging schools, under policies that at times frustrate them and limit their autonomy. Resoundingly, their answer is through the community they maintain with their colleagues. Teacher community and collaboration is critical to cultivating the notions of practice we aim to nurture. Teacher educators can help new teachers to understand this and also support their efforts at building and sustaining this kind of community. Highlighting examples of community and collective action helps us to productively think about the ways we can bring practitioner voices into larger policy conversations and preserve complex and sustaining notions of practice.

CHAPTER 4

Voices from the Field

Thus far, we have considered practice from a range of perspectives, thinking about it through the scholarly literature and in relation to our own work in teacher education. In Chapter 1, we laid the groundwork for the rest of the book by exploring the multiple meanings and uses of practice. We began and ended with an idea that, while it seems obvious, is far too often sidelined in education policy conversations: teaching fundamentally involves being with people. Envisioning teaching as a set of decontextualized practices is generally not very useful to teachers. Richer notions of practice are needed to support educators who see classrooms as complex and always changing spaces, and who seek opportunities to continually learn and grow in relation to these contexts.

In Chapter 2, we consider the global trend toward practice-based teacher education and how it has continued to evolve around the world. We explore both the historical and current instantiations of practice-based teaching to raise critical questions about the role of practice in the preparation of teachers. We argue against divorcing practice from theory and research, even as we recognize the value of grounded approaches to integrating practice-based perspectives. We conclude with the need for more robust ideas about pedagogy to supplant the scaled-down versions of practice that are commonly taken up around the world.

In Chapter 3, we argue that a critical interrogation of practice provides an invaluable window into marketization and privatization as it impacts and redefines teachers' work. We show how asking questions of practice helps us to think about the ways prioritizing profits and scalability over educational quality undermines both economic and democratic purposes of education. Through holding onto complex notions of practice and resisting impoverished ideas about the nature of teachers' work, teachers and teacher educators can speak back to these trends and gain a stronger voice in these conversations.

Across the chapters, we see that while the term practice appears to be neutral, it is actually deeply value-laden and political. We see that discourses of practice are used to spread policy ideas on a global scale, to claim expertise, to bargain for entry into policymaking conversations, to empower or disempower teachers, to discredit or support schools of education, and more. We show that, regardless of how one understands and enacts practice, practice is always about much more than what teachers do in the classroom. Perhaps this is why the word practice has caused so much debate and controversy in the teacher education community.

In this chapter, we turn to a conversation among scholars about practice in university-based teacher education and professional development programs. In order to gain a clearer sense of how educators and scholars understand the term practice, we conducted interviews with seven scholars, from the United States, Norway, and Switzerland, who have written extensively about practice. Marilyn Cochran-Smith is professor emerita at the Lynch School of Education and Human Development at Boston College and Professor II with the Faculty of Education at the Norwegian University of Science and Technology. Urban Fraefel is professor emeritus of the School of Education at the University of Applied Sciences and Arts of Northwestern Switzerland. Megan Franke is professor at the University of California Los Angeles. Pam

Grossman is dean emerita and professor at the University of Pennsylvania Graduate School of Education. Ilana (Lani) Horn is professor at the Peabody School at Vanderbilt University. Inga Staal Jenset is associate professor at the University of Oslo. Finally, Kirsti Klette is professor and center director of the Nordic Centre of Excellence Quality in Nordic Teaching at the University of Oslo.

In these interviews, we asked the scholars to talk about their definitions and understandings of practice and practice-based teacher education, and to think with us about how their ideas have changed over time and how these ideas helped to shape their teacher education and professional development programs. We read additional articles they had written and looked across the interviews for themes and insights. We saw how these scholars have used their own constantly evolving sense of practice to direct their work as teacher educators or leaders of programs that support teachers' ongoing professional growth.

The idea of practice has become a lightning rod in conversations about teacher education in the United States and the UK, with the idea of "core practices," in particular, sparking controversy. At the conclusion of one of our interviews, a US teacher educator reflected on the use of the term "practice" in teacher education and the controversy that has, at times, enveloped the conversation.

> For me it's a cautionary tale that we have seen in our field many times. The terms and words we use take on meanings that aren't intended and take us down paths of not talking to each other in ways that aren't helpful. I feel like it's just created an unfortunate divide.

We do not intend to resolve the divides and disagreements around practice either in this chapter or in this book. Instead, we argue for the value of reclaiming debates and conversations about practice. We found ourselves incredibly energized and engaged as we conducted and analyzed these interviews. All of the scholars were grappling in fundamental, interesting, and instructive ways with the challenge of defining practice and ways of thinking about and bridging the theory–practice divide. None of the scholars held a singular definition of practice, and despite some divergences, there were significant overlaps and commonalities across their reflections. As we thought about these interviews in the context of this book, we were struck by the importance of holding these conversations about practice, given the precarity of our current moment across the globe and the tightening of regulations and control of teachers' work.

In that vein, we aim here to present contemporary ideas in conversation with each other to deepen our understanding of the term "practice" and to help us look toward the future of how to prepare teachers in ways that are transformative and humane. In thinking across these interviews, we ask: What are the underlying principles and ideas that shape teacher educators' definitions and understandings of practice? How do understandings of practice lead to the design and enactment of teacher education and professional development programs? How might we structure conversations about practice within and across programs that are productive and potentially transformative? We address each of these questions in turn in the sections that follow.

Defining Practice

Practice as Interactional and Relational

We were interested to learn how each of the scholars defined practice. All of the scholars, in their own way, spoke of practice as an interactional achievement. Practice was not something the teacher did, or something that could be located in the teacher. Rather, it was something achieved through the interactions of teachers with their colleagues, students, families, communities, classroom space, textbooks, curriculum mandates, social structures, and more. Each of the scholars we spoke with proposed definitions of practice grounded in relationships.

As Pam Grossman explained, "the work of teaching is what you know and who you are as a person. The students that you have in the classroom have a lot of influence on the practices that you engage in." She continued:

> Practice-based teacher education is not just about the practical work you do in schools. Not just about clinical practice. But also deeply embedded with knowing, knowing your content, knowing about the students you teach, knowing the purposes of education, and how those again, influence the approaches that you then would take in a classroom and then how you enact those.

To Pam, teaching begins with knowing students; her understanding of practice is relational, embedded in that knowledge.

Lani Horn studies how teachers continue to learn across their professional careers through carefully honed professional development. She articulated her understandings of practice as follows:

> I mean, one of the things that I think is really interesting about working with in-service teachers that's distinct from working with preservice teachers is that they already have a very deep and embodied and lived sense of practice. And all of the teachers we work with … have five years of experience, and many of them have more like 15, 20, 25 so we have to think about practice in a pretty deep way. We are not the purveyors of practice. We are partners in inquiry into their practice. So it's a kind of different framing of what we're up to as teacher educators.

Situating her idea of practice as "very anthropologically rooted," Lani went on to explain the way she viewed all practice as an interactional achievement, noting that teacher knowledge is inherently partial. As she states,

> practice is tangled, teacher practice is irreducibly situative and relational … it doesn't exist within a person. It's an interactional accomplishment, and therefore teacher knowledge is inherently partial.

For Lani, practice cannot be understood apart from the interactions that surround it. A teacher's practice might be understood through a conversation about how she uses notebooks in her classroom and what they might mean for a student coming into her classroom with particular strengths and vulnerabilities around that practice or an acceptance or resistance to using notebooks in a teacher-directed manner. These ideas, or practices, are understood through conversations, contexts, people, and the emotions and expectations surrounding the interactions.

An understanding of practice as co-constructed with others, including student teachers, and as situationally made and remade over time, also came up in the conversation with Megan Franke. Megan talked about the resistance she and her colleagues faced in their program, particularly from secondary education students, who found the program's idea of practice to be more about controlling as opposed to relating. Students challenged the focus on practice as contrary to their goals of social justice, even as Megan and her colleagues worked hard to foreground structural and relational aspects of inequality. Megan explained that she and her colleagues had to come up with different ways of talking and thinking about practice and, importantly, needed to do this in conversation with students.

> I think we did get to a relational way [of thinking], and the way that we got there was that there are advantages to naming some aspects of the work [of teaching] and trying to think about, what does it mean to be good at that and what does it look like to be good at that? And how do we build

> into that issues of race and racism, histories of communities, ideas about the ways in which school structures are shaping what happens for young people. I think their worry is that all of that's on the outside of practice, and you do practices separate from all of that. And so we tried to think about how to shift that conversation away from this notion that practice is a single thing somebody does to something that's about the work that we do, and that the work we do is deeply situated in schooling, society, history … . So I think it was just finding different ways to honor what they did really care about, and to try and not devolve into something that was isolating particular things we do and thinking more about the work we do together.

Megan and her colleagues were already thinking deeply about the kinds of structural inequalities that their students raised as reasons for objecting to their ideas about practice. Rather than trying to explain this or justify their stance, however, the teacher educators met the students with curiosity, listened to their concerns, revisited their own ideas, and worked with students toward a collaboratively constructed vision of practice that allowed everyone to move forward. This collaborative work stands in direct contrast to the idea of assessing and determining best practices and demonstrating those practices to students for their enactment in classrooms. It demonstrates an understanding of practice that is profoundly relational.

Practice as Grounded in Community and Place

The idea that practice is always an interactional achievement went hand in hand with the idea that practice is always rooted in a physical place or context; recognizing and engaging substantively with this context was key to the robust ideas of practice that emerged in these interviews. For the scholars we spoke with, taking practice seriously meant much more than just spending additional time in schools. They lamented the way the "turn to practice" in teacher education is often thought of in these overly simplistic terms. Marilyn Cochran-Smith explained:

> So, you know, Relay is an example of practice-based teacher education, I think they would say, and they could lay it out for you and say, here's why. And all of the teacher residencies, even though they're really different from one another, they share more of an emphasis [on being] in the schools. Some people will say that's practice-based teacher education, because people are in the schools more and we're putting the practice part sooner, stronger, upfront. That has been certainly referred to as practice-based teacher education. So, you know, in some states like Texas, where so many people are prepared in programs that are not connected to universities or colleges, a big percentage of the new teachers in the state, I think they would say that's a focus on practice.

Marilyn situated this view of practice-based teacher education in contrast to her own more complex view of practice and school placement, but as she astutely pointed out,

> I can't say practice-based teacher education is only this because this is more consistent with my views. I can say practice-based teacher education is defined very differently by different people.

The other scholars we spoke with shared versions of this critique. They also went beyond, and indeed were often critical of, simply advocating for more time in schools as a way to improve teacher practice. Instead, they thought carefully about the structure of fieldwork, its relationship to the university classroom, and the way that they, as teacher educators, modeled engagement with and responsiveness to school and global communities. In other words, their definitions of practice were deeply considerate of and responsive to the places where they were located.

The UCLA program Megan worked with and directed made the decision to embed the program in the community, learning with and from community members, teachers and students in the schools in order to make decisions about how and what to teach. While some practice-based programs imagine simply spending more time in schools brings student teachers closer to practice, Megan and her colleagues framed time in school differently. They wanted to be part of, accountable to, and in conversation with their school community as well as the broader community surrounding the school. In doing so, they aimed to cultivate a robust notion of practice with students, where engagement with communities was central to their work as teachers.

Megan described the decision of her program, led by Jeannie Oakes at the time, to locate their content and pedagogy courses in the primary and secondary schools as a way to invest more deeply in their Los Angeles community. Their decision came after the riots in Los Angeles in response to the Rodney King beating by police officers. Other programs may have retreated back to the university to protect students from potential violence in the broader community. In contrast, their teacher education program moved classes into the community and began to develop ways to work more closely with teachers and schools where student teachers were placed for their field experiences. Megan immediately noticed the difference in their conversations about practice with their students and among themselves, and has seen how this shift has persisted over time. Remembering the day after the first election of Donald Trump, she described how, as teacher educators, they were uniquely able to respond, because they were working at the school site:

> It was a low-income school with lots of immigrant young people and the panic on these little people's faces, I will never forget. And my students saw that, and we got to talk about that and think about, well, now what are we going to do in math class, given that this just happened today? And so when you're at a school site doing the work of teacher

> education, you can't ignore the structures of school in any way. And so that work helped shift our teacher ed program in ways that we had conversations.

Located in the school and immersed in practice, the conversations during their teacher education classes shifted directly in response to their students' emotions and experiences. The decision to locate their teacher education program in schools and communities, and to pay close attention to and engage with what mattered in those communities at a given moment, profoundly shaped their understandings and enactments of practice.

Practice as Complex

Through her experience as a teacher educator in secondary English/Language Arts methods courses, Pam found that prospective teachers insisted on learning practices they could bring to their classrooms the next day. They asked her, "What do I actually do when I'm in a classroom? How can I put these ideas into practice?" She explained that she found it difficult to find examples of classrooms where teachers were enacting the kinds of practices she and her colleagues felt that the prospective teachers needed to learn. As she explained,

> It's hard to find those mentors who are really embodying the kind of practice that we're teaching about. I felt like we couldn't leave it all to the field. And that too often was the problem. For example, Ken [Zeichner] has talked a lot about the fact that the experience in schools washes out whatever kind of progressive efforts the university teacher education courses try to make.

For Pam, the solution to this was to bring "the teaching of practice into the context of the university, while working with schools and teachers to try to bridge that gap."

Kirsti Klette and Inga Staal Jenset reached a similar conclusion. They worried that the definition of practice in Norway rested too heavily on what occurred in the field and wanted to complicate that idea by bringing ideas from primary and secondary classrooms into the university. Kirsti tells the story of how her understanding of practice grew over time through her work as a teacher educator in Norway, her work with international scholars, and discussions with her own colleagues that stretched across time. The conception of learning practice in teacher education as connected to spending time in schools is common across the globe, a view that Kirsti embraced in her initial years as a teacher educator.

> [When I began as a teacher educator], I had a quite simple vision and understanding of practice. That meant, you know, the amount of weeks the students were out in the real schools, and in that sense, we have a strong tradition for having this sort of component in teacher education. … When we redesigned our program, we realized that practice should not be something that was privileged to the placement periods [in clinical settings in schools], but it should influence the program as a whole, in terms of the content, in terms of the courses, in terms of the readings, in terms of the assignments. One of the basic pillars in our redesign model was to make a stronger alignment between the practices they learned in the field placement and what they learned through the campus courses and the assignments.

While it may sound simple, the process of redefining practice from spending time in primary and secondary classrooms to studying practices in the university classroom is actually complex and one that Kirsti and her colleague, Inga, have worked on for years as they have sought to bring coherence to their teacher education program and to teacher education programs across Norway.

Practice as Intertwined with Theory

As we read through our interviews with scholars, it became clear that each scholar was, in their own way, constructing and then grappling with a perceived divide between theory and practice. The debate about theory and practice has been persistent across history and is still considered a central problem for teacher educators across the world (cf., Korthagen, 2010). Clandinin (1995) calls this narrative the "sacred theory-practice story," explaining that in her own teacher education classes in Western Canada, where she was introduced to the profession, she was "filled with theory that I could then apply to my teaching practice, first as a student teacher and, soon after, as a newly qualified teacher" (pp. 28–9). As a student teacher, she understood the need to pretend that the theories were useful to her practice and that she needed a "cover story" to convince her university instructors that she knew the theory and could apply it in practice. Many years later as a teacher educator, Clandinin joined with university colleagues, classroom teachers, and student teachers to design an alternative teacher education program at that same university. She writes powerfully about the ways they rethought the relationship between theory and practice and their continual process of re-storying the theory–practice divide toward transformative possibilities.

In our interview with Marilyn Cochran-Smith, she echoed these themes, although her focus was on the relationships between knowledge and practice and, in particular, the kinds of knowledge and the sources for that knowledge that are used in the preparation of teachers and teacher professional development. Marilyn has written over the years with Susan Lytle about the relationship between knowledge and practice. She discussed her large and encompassing view of practice that breaks through the theory–practice divide and comes from this work. As Marilyn explains,

> Practice is a much, much bigger notion that has to do with what [teachers] do, of course, but also how they think about what they do and the interpretive frameworks they use to

> make sense of what they're doing, to make sense of the problems, to even say what is a problem. How do I know what's a problem? How do I define it? All of that is part of practice, the way they form relationships with parents and communities and other teachers and other professional colleagues.

In Marilyn and Susan Lytle's conception of practice (e.g., Cochran-Smith and Lytle, 1999), it is imperative that teachers bring their interpretive frameworks or theories to their inquiry into practice. They argue that practices cannot be understood apart from these frameworks, in much the same way that the other scholars explain that practice is always understood in relationship to people and place. Marilyn continues by discussing her broad understanding of practice as grounded in the myriad connections between practice, knowledge, and justice.

> When you tie it together with what you assume about the relationship [between] knowledge and practice, and then tie that to purpose, equity, justice, effectiveness, achievement, all those things, then it is everything, in a way. So I'm not saying practice is everything, but practice is way bigger than forty-nine actions that teachers take.

This understanding of practice stands in direct contrast to the forty-nine strategies for teaching that Lemov (2010) describes in *Teach Like a Champion*, which are generally understood as devoid of theory and focused on the daily actions of teachers.

Faculty in schools of education often face colleagues who claim that teaching methods courses are atheoretical; as a result, those courses and, at times, those faculty have a lesser status in the universities. In the UK, the move to locate teacher training in primary and secondary schools was in response to the idea that teacher education should be entirely practical rather than informed by theory. These ideas stand in stark contrast to the beliefs of the scholars we spoke with, who all understood and articulated the ways that theory is integrated in practice.

For instance, in our interview with Pam, she talked about the dissonance she experienced early in her career as she was teaching methods courses. Methods courses were routinely looked down on or seen as a waste of time by colleagues, even as students regularly cited them as some of the most helpful courses they took in preparing to teach.

> As somebody who's taught methods and repeatedly was told by students that this was the most helpful course that they took in teacher education, I was always struck by [the idea that methods courses were a waste of time] and wondering why it was that practice got … so little respect and such low status within the university. And that's not just teacher education. The aspects of legal education that are taught by adjuncts and get the least attention have to do with legal writing aspects of the law that actually involve the doing of law. So, you know, it really struck me that this is not just a problem in teacher education, it's a broader problem. And yet again, as I said, it's in dissonance with what novice teachers often are asking for, which is more help with what do I actually do when I'm in a classroom? How can I put these ideas into practice? And so it was really that divide between theory and practice that I think motivated my interest in looking more at what does it mean to teach practice in the context of a university-based teacher education program? And I think a lot of effort went into improving the quality of clinical practice.

Pam later elaborated on this point, reiterating the way that theory and practice are intertwined, "Everything I do, all the practices I focus on include theory and helping students understand why you might make some of those choices, why you might engage."

In many Western European countries and throughout much of the world, teacher education programs have traditionally focused on educational theory. This has led some countries to turn to practice, or to work to make more explicit the connection between theory and practice. In discussing his understanding of the theory–practice relationship, Urban Fraefel explained the English word "practice" has several synonyms in German, including *praxis*, which is thought of as the opposite of theory, and *praktik*, which is something a person does, like classroom management. He went on to note that his own ideas are that practice necessarily integrates theory, rather than its opposite. Toward that end, he describes the shifts his program in Switzerland has made to support teacher learning as follows:

> Learning is rooted in concrete action and teachers therefore preferably take their own activity as the starting point for learning processes. This aspect of empowerment seems very important to us because we want teachers to work on improving their practices even after completing teacher training; for example, we want to initiate student teachers into this work on practices. We have more or less broken with the teacher training strategy of reflection that has dominated for decades, because although reflection on one's own actions is desirable, in our experience it usually remains quite unspecific, focuses too much on deficits, and is carried out too often just for the sake of the teacher trainers, whereas work on practices is specific and solution and success oriented.

To Urban, the concept of practice includes theory and guides action in classrooms. During our interview, Urban drew out a pack of cards from his backpack that were developed at a neighboring university. Each card had a core practice written on the front and an explanation on the back. This deck of cards is a useful tool, Urban explained, for focusing teachers' attention on practices and prompting conversation. Contrasting this notion of practice to "best practices" he elaborated, "so our practice is never best, an absolute decontextualized best practice. So this aspect of adapting it to the actual situation, not only in application, but also in the understanding and the internal conceptualization." Teacher educators use the cards in creative and adaptive ways to make practices visible to the students and respond to the concerns they bring about their own developing practices as educators, supporting the integration of theory and practice.

How Do Definitions of Practice Shape Program Designs?

The complex, layered ways in which the scholars we spoke with understood practice shaped their decision-making processes and their ideas about how to design teacher education and professional learning programs. In other words, the way they defined practice shaped the ways they engaged in and reflected on their practices as teacher educators. In this next section, we highlight a few of the striking examples they offered of the ways they enacted their ideas about practice in their work as teacher educators.

Developing and Using Tools for Looking and Thinking

As reflected in the prior section, everyone we spoke with thought of practice as incredibly complex. Sorting through this complexity in ways that recognize teachers' knowledge of context and support their ongoing growth is key to teacher education and professional development. The scholars we spoke with found that one productive entry point for these kinds of conversations is gathering and reflecting on data from practice in collaboration with teachers. From this lens, the teacher educator becomes a partner in identifying, gathering, and analyzing data to support teachers in their own professional development and growth.

For example, Lani and her team have developed sophisticated methods for recording practice in order to prompt teachers to reflect on their decisions during their teaching. This useful lens, developed over time and in response to ongoing work with educators, allows teachers to gain insight into their own practice that they might miss through simple observation. Working with Ben Rydal Shapiro, they have developed a way to connect video of teachers' practice to spatial mappings of teachers' movement throughout the classroom. Lani explained: "We took to scale measurements of their classrooms, including their furniture, and we are able to represent the flow of their lesson through their movement, and that's all hyperlinked to video." This videotaping and the teachers' own inquiry into their questions of practice have allowed Lani and her team to capture "ineffable, ephemeral aspects of practice ... things like pacing, things like your position, when you do certain things, things like, who do you talk to first? Things like when you approach a group of kids, how much listening are you doing and how much talking are you doing?"

Through their collaborative viewing of the video, teachers gain new insights into their practice. What makes this teacher education practice powerful is that Lani and her team are able to talk to teachers about their decisions in real time. As she explains,

> And one of the arguments I've made many times is that part of the complexity of supporting teacher learning is that our opportunities for talking to teachers about their practice are almost always asynchronous from the actual act of practice, which is different from other professions, right? Like, if I'm a surgeon, I can observe and talk to a more experienced surgeon who is operating at the same time. If I'm a pilot, we can go up and, you know, I can take over the controls at a certain point. [In teaching], we don't have that same kind of real time, parallel opportunity to learn.

In her debriefing with one of the teachers in her professional development work, the teacher told a story about a time that

Lani noticed something about a student and raised a question. The teacher realized that she didn't know that student, who had successfully hidden himself from her for the whole year. She shifted her practice and explained to Lani, "and when you asked me those questions, I realized I knew nothing about him … I don't do that anymore. I don't let kids be invisible to me." Allowing teachers to shift their practice based on data and to see and hear the students in their classrooms is critical; a focus on and respect for teachers' practices allows this to happen.

Embedding Teaching in Communities

In Megan's interview, we saw that locating the UCLA teacher education program in the surrounding community rather than the university campus was an intentional and powerful statement by the program leaders, reflecting their understanding of practice as larger and grounded in place. It also illustrated their strong commitment to going beyond using schools and communities as sites for student teaching, engaging in deep and authentic ways. Megan explained that in addition to moving their program into the community, they made the decision to extend their master's program from one to two years; in their second year, the students in their program were first-year teachers in their partner schools. This meant that there were partner teachers, first-year teachers, student teachers, and faculty all working together in the same school. In addition to locating mathematics methods classes in the schools, Megan worked closely with a partner teacher—who was an elementary classroom teacher—to design opportunities for the university students and elementary students to learn together. Reflecting on this experience, Megan described her understanding of what it means to become a teacher as grounded in practice:

> So for me, it's about becoming a particular person as a teacher, right? I want them to have some skills and abilities

> around listening to young people and hearing what they have to say and knowing what it looks like and feels like to build on those ideas. Yes, but mostly what I want them to leave our program with is being people who think about teaching as a relational and situational and structural and societal act, and that you never stop learning to teach and that it's a collective act. So, you don't learn to teach by yourself. You learn to teach with your students. You learn to teach because of the artifacts you surround yourself with. You learn to teach because of the people. And so I want them to know how to build coalitions of people to help them do the work they want to do, and to help them do work that challenges the ways in which schooling restricts opportunities for their young people.

For Megan, learning to teach went beyond learning particular practices; learning to teach meant becoming a certain kind of person who works in coalition with others and in deep partnership with the community.

Providing Opportunities for Practice and Mastery

Over time, teacher educators have searched for ways to teach classroom practices in university classrooms that go beyond delivering lectures. Magdalene Lampert and her colleagues (2013) write about the importance of rehearsals or opportunities to practice instructional activities that lead to ambitious instruction in their university courses. Teacher educators, like Pam, discovered that prospective teachers needed more scaffolded, deliberate opportunities to learn complex practices.

Drawing on her experiences as a teacher and teacher educator, Pam has embraced a conception of practice-based teacher education that places teaching and learning about practices at the center of learning to teach, while holding onto a larger, theoretically grounded vision of practice. In a study of professional education across three professions (education, clergy, and clinical psychology), designed to understand how the relational aspects of teaching practice can be taught, Pam and her team (2009) developed a framework for describing practice that includes representations, decomposition, and approximations of practice in professional education. Representations include the use of videotaping and also the use of artifacts of teaching such as lesson plans, student work or observational notes.

Decomposition of practice is the identification of the components of teaching that can be taught in a focused way, so that students can attend to each component. As they write, "we refer to this work as the 'decomposition' of practice—breaking down complex practice into its constituent parts for the purposes of teaching and learning. Decomposing practice enables students both to 'see' and enact elements of practice more effectively" (Grossman et al., 2009, p. 2069). This notion of practice rests on the idea that practices are discrete and can be broken down into constituent parts that can then be reassembled once they are learned, emphasizing both its complexity and also the coherence of the practice. Critical to this view of practice is the notion that practices are teachable rather than objects of study.

The third component of the framework is approximations of practice or trying out practices in university classrooms before taking them into the field. As Pam explained,

> So I think seeing the ways in which other professions brought these elements of practice into the university-based classroom and then really focusing students' attention on them, engaging them in the kinds of approximations of practice that I write about, giving them really tailored feedback, and then you could see them get better.

Pam went on to explain the affordances brought by videotaping teachers' practice, especially because they could see progress in how the teachers enacted practices that they had not previously been able to articulate. As she explained,

> I think that was the other thing that was really striking to me is just like watching in the moment how and this is when we went to videotaping is like, I don't even know how to describe this in words, how you can see people gaining confidence and getting better at these fairly complex practices. That really made me come back and really change my methods course.

In addition to seeing how teachers learned by practicing components of practice with specific feedback, Pam and her colleagues found that the videotaping allowed them to talk about ideas that are often difficult to put into words. At the same time, breaking practices into components gave them opportunities to create new vocabulary for teaching practices. A definition of practice as complex, yet able to be broken down into components and then practiced in university classrooms, shifted the pedagogical practices that Pam used in her own methods classes and in the teacher education programs she has helped to shape. In sum, her focus has been on acknowledging the complexity of practice while developing pedagogies that make the practices teachable.

Cultivating an Inquiry Stance

A question that came up for us repeatedly in writing this book—and then emerged again across our conversations with scholars—was how to manage the incredible complexity of practice. A tension emerges. On the one hand, we need to hold onto the complexity and messiness of practice; this is especially critical in today's policy environment where the work of teaching is viewed in simplistic and reductive terms that undermine teacher autonomy and eclipse student learning. On the other hand, we need to support new and practicing teachers with models and tools that help them grasp and think through the intricacies of their practice. In other words, how can we hold the complexity of teaching while simultaneously supporting teachers to see through this complexity in ways that support student learning and growth?

Cultivating an inquiry stance has emerged as one powerful answer to this question. Rooted in Marilyn Cochran-Smith and Susan Lytle's foundational work on teacher inquiry, centering teacher education around inquiry is a powerful way to hold the complexity of practice while respecting and supporting the professionalism of teachers. Marilyn's definition of practice is broad and expansive. As with others we spoke to, she thinks of practice as more than something teachers do, emphasizing the relational and context-based components.

> Practice is what teachers do and how they think about what they do, and how they work with others. It's all those things, that's what practice is about. And so if you're going to build teacher education programs or professional development programs, and that's your view of practice, then you have to think about how can we focus on that? How can we create the context—social, organizational, intellectual—how can we create these contexts to support teacher development in terms of [seeing] practice in that broad, broad way?

As she discussed her vision for building these contexts that support broad notions of practice, Marilyn turned to inquiry, highlighting that everyone must come as a learner—not just the preservice or in-service teacher—for us to truly understand and improve practice.

> I think that programs that try to, as we've said for years, programs that see everybody as a learner and an inquirer, the student teacher, the cooperating teacher, the university supervisor, the university coursework teacher, the head of teacher education, all those people as inquirers and learners

> who have a practice, who are engaged in practice, everybody's a learner. Nobody knows everything. There's never an end. It's never a done deal. And people come together and inquire in a community, in an inquiry community, and what are they inquiring about? Well, in the broadest sense, they're inquiring about practice and all of its dimensions.

Marilyn made clear the connection between knowledge and practice, clarifying the sorts of epistemological questions that come part and parcel with a more complicated view of teacher practice.

> And we talked about the data of practice. If we want practitioners to collect the data of practice based on questions they have or problems they're posing, what would count as data? What is the data of practice? And of course, if you have a very narrow view, like my professor did when I was in undergrad, then if you have a very narrow view of practice, you would only collect some kinds of observational data about what teachers did in classrooms, not unlike the process-product research that was all the rage in those days. But if you have this much broader notion of practice, what data are teachers going to collect? What is the data of practice? Well, it's a whole lot of what they do. It's their kids' work, it's what their kids say. It's their interactions with parents. It's the materials that they look at, you know? I mean, it's just a whole different world. And I see these questions about practice as central to all of these topics. It's not the only concept that's important, obviously, but the relationship between knowledge and practice is so intricately, intensely interwoven that practice pulls so many other things in.

For Marilyn, taking an inquiry stance means supporting teachers in always getting underneath the surface, always trying to unpack what is happening, such that they themselves hold and continually reconstruct complex notions of practice.

Conclusion: How Do We Support Conversations About Practice?

As we reflect on these interviews and conclude the book, we are struck by the commonalities in our interviews far more than the divides that too often characterize conversations about practice in teacher education. We noticed that each scholar approached the discussion with a spirit of humility and understanding that our knowledge of teaching is always partial as it is rooted in interactions and relationships. Lani Horn prompted us to think again about Britzman's (1991) idea that "practice makes practice," reinforcing the importance of practicing as intrinsic to knowing, listening to, and learning about the meanings teachers make before we introduce new theories and ideas. We were reminded, from our own experiences, of the importance of dialogue and conversations with colleagues, including classroom teachers, as a way to make sense of ideas, to address conflicting notions, and to create new programs. We heard a resistance to the low status of the profession and a profound respect for the complexity of practice, including the need to take an inquiry stance to understand what is underneath practices. Finally, each person stated a commitment to justice as key to rethinking and redesigning teacher education as inextricably linked to the role of practice in teacher education.

Throughout this book, we have argued that an interrogation of practice underscores how teachers' professionalism is at risk on a global scale. Just as an exploration of practice brings the problem of teacher professionalism and autonomy into focus, it can also help us to imagine solutions or pathways forward. We find inspiration in the ideas we have introduced throughout the book. Fugitive pedagogy illustrates how teachers and teacher educators act on their beliefs in the face of oppressive systems, providing a blueprint for taking courageous action. Collective action and community offer ways for teachers to hold onto and nurture robust notions of practice, and to create the conditions for enacting these practices. Engaging in conversations about the complexity of practice and the responses of teacher education and professional development programs—even when disagreements arise—helps to nurture the robust definitions of practice that speak back to the de-professionalization of teachers. We conclude not by arguing for a particular definition or version of practice, but rather by advocating for diverse, varied, complex perspectives, putting them in conversation with each other, in order to resist impoverished notions of teachers' practice and teachers' work. As we have shown throughout this book, complex notions of practice are critical to our goal of finding ways to dignify teachers' work and support student learning. We can ask each other: How do we nurture these debates and conversations, recognizing their import and their broader context? Who are the stakeholders we want to bring into conversation with one another? What conversations do we need to hold and how will these dialogues allow us to address the precarity of teaching as a profession? What role can teacher education play in creating sustainable and intellectually vibrant work for teachers?

We conclude with an image of teaching that Maxine Greene (1997, p. 23) gave us almost thirty years ago and is even more relevant today.

> What is meant by teaching as possibility in dark and constraining times? It is a matter of awakening and empowering today's young people to name, to reflect, to imagine, and to act with more and more concrete responsibility in an increasingly multifarious world. At once, it is a matter of enabling them to remain in touch with dread and desire, with the smell of lilacs and the taste of a peach. The light may be uncertain and flickering; but teachers in their lives and works have the remarkable capacity to make it shine in all sorts of corners and, perhaps, to move newcomers to join with others and transform.

Like Greene, and as we have shown throughout the book, we believe that teaching is complex, and sometimes daunting, work that requires that we acknowledge the darkness, while staying in touch with the moments of sweetness, light, and possibility. We wonder, what would it take to design teacher education programs that nurture this kind of practice? We know that as teacher educators we need to keep the concept of practice in our domain. Holding conversations and debates about how to keep practice rich, complex, relational, and vibrant is a critical first step.

REFERENCES

Alegre, M. A., and G. Ferrer (2010), "School Regimes and Education Equity: Some Insights Based on PISA 2006," *British Educational Research Journal*, 36 (3): 433–61.

Anderson, L. M. (2019), "Private Interests in a Public Profession: Teacher Education and Racial Capitalism," *Teachers College Record*, 121: 1–37.

Anderson, L. M., and J. Stillman (2012), "Student Teaching's Contribution to Preservice Teacher Development: A Review of Research Focused on the Preparation of Teachers for Urban and High-Needs Contexts," *Review of Educational Research*, 83 (1): 3–69.

Anyon, J. (2005), *Radical Possibilities: Public Policy, Urban Education, and a New Social Movement*, New York: Routledge.

Ball, D. L., and D. K. Cohen (1999), "Developing Practice, Developing Practitioners: Towards a Practice-Based Theory of Professional Education," in L. Darling-Hammond and G. Sykes (eds.), *Teaching as the Learning Profession: Handbook of Policy and Practice*, 3–32, San Francisco: Jossey-Bass.

Ball, D. L., and F. M. Forzani (2009), "The Work of Teaching and the Challenge for Teacher Education," *Journal of Teacher Education*, 60 (5): 497–511.

Ball, S. J. (2007), *Education plc: Understanding Private Sector Participation in Public Sector Education*, London: Routledge.

Ball, S. J. (2012), *Global Education Inc.: New Policy Networks and the Neo-Liberal Imaginary*, London: Routledge.

Bartlett, L., P. Crookes, and C. Stokes (2002), "Marketization and Education: The Effects on Equity and Access," *Comparative Education*, 38 (1): 21–38.

Beauchamp, G., L. Clarke, M. Hulme, and J. Murray (2013), *Research and Teacher Education: The BERA-RSA Inquiry. Policy and Practice within the United Kingdom*, Project Report, London: British Educational Research Association.

Bennell, P. (2024), "An Education Revolution: The Privatization of Schooling in Capital City Conurbations in Sub-Saharan Africa," *International Journal of Educational Development*, 105: 102988.

Bennett, T., L. Grossberg, and M. Morris (2005). *New Keywords. A Revised Vocabulary of Culture and Society*, Oxford: Blackwell Publishing.

Berliner, D. C. (1975), *The Beginning Teacher Evaluation Study: Overview and Selected Findings*, San Francisco, CA: Far West Regional Laboratory for Educational Research and Development.

Bertram, C., and L. Rusznyak (2024), "Navigating Tensions in Designing a Curriculum That Prepares Preservice Teachers for School-Based Learning," *Education as Change*, 28: 1–23.

Best, S., and S. Hartman (2005), "Fugitive Justice," *Representations*, 92 (1): 1–115.

Braaten, M. (2018), "Persistence of the Two-Worlds Pitfall: Learning to Teach within and across Settings," *Science Education*, 103: 61–91.

Brewer, T. J. (2014), "Accelerated Burnout: How Teach For America's Academic Impact Model and Theoretical Culture of Accountability Can Foster Disillusionment Among Its Corps Members," *Educational Studies*, 50 (3): 246–63.

Britzman, D. P. (1991), "Decentering Discourses in Teacher Education: Or, the Unleashing of Unpopular Things," *Journal of Education*, 173 (3): 60–80.

Britzman, D. P. (2003), *Practice Makes Practice: A Critical Study of Learning to Teach*, Revised ed., Albany: State University of New York Press.

Brockenbrough, E. (2024), *Learning While Black and Queer: Understanding the Educational Experiences of Black LGBTQ+ Youth*, Cambridge, MA: Harvard Education Press.

Brown, K. D. (2013), "Trouble on My Mind: Toward a Framework of Humanizing Critical Sociocultural Knowledge for Teaching and Teacher Education," *Race Ethnicity and Education*, 16 (3): 316–38.

Brown, W. (2015), *Undoing the Demos: Neoliberalism's Stealth Revolution*, Cambridge, MA: MIT Press.

Buras, K. L. (2011), "Race, Charter Schools, and Conscious Capitalism: On the Spatial Politics of Whiteness as Property (and the Unconscionable Assault on Black New Orleans)," *Harvard Educational Review*, 81 (2): 290–317.

Buras, K. L. (2013), "New Orleans Education Reform: A Guide for Cities or a Warning for Communities? (Grassroots Lessons

Learned, 2005–2012)," *Berkeley Review of Education*, 4 (1): 123–60.

Buras, K. L. (2015), *Charter Schools, Race, and Urban Space: Where the Market Meets Grassroots Resistance*, New York: Routledge.

Buras, K. L. (2016), "The Mass Termination of Black Veteran Teachers in New Orleans: Cultural Politics, the Education Market, and Its Consequences," *The Educational Forum*, 80 (2): 154–70.

Burn, K., and T. Mutton (2015), "Beginning Teachers' Learning: Making Experience Count," London: Routledge.

Calabrese Barton, A., E. Tan, and D. J. Birmingham (2020), "Rethinking High-Leverage Practices in Justice-Oriented Ways," *Journal of Teacher Education*, 71 (4): 477–94.

Carini, P. (1986), *Prospect's Documentary Process*, Bennington, VT: Prospect School Center.

Childress, S. (2016), "From Generation to Generation: Fifteen Years of Educational Entrepreneurship," in F. M. Hess and M. Q. McShane (eds.), *Educational Entrepreneurship Today*, 11–34, Cambridge, MA: Harvard University Press.

Clandinin, D. J. (1995), "Still Learning to Teach," in T. Russell and F. Korthagen (eds.), *Teachers Who Teach Teachers*, 25–31, London: Routledge.

Cochran-Smith, M. (2020), "Relocating Teacher Preparation to New Graduate Schools of Education." *The New Educator*, 17 (1): 1–20.

Cochran-Smith, M., and S. L. Lytle (1999), "Relationships of Knowledge and Practice: Teacher Learning in Communities," *Review of Research in Education*, 24 (1): 249–305.

Cochran-Smith, M., and S. L. Lytle (2019), *Inquiry as Stance: Practitioner Research for the Next Generation. Practitioners Inquiry*. New York: Teachers College Press.

Cochran-Smith, M., E. S. Keefe, M. C. Carney, J. G. Sánchez, M. Olivo, and R. J. Smith (2020), "Teacher Preparation at New Graduate Schools of Education: Studying a Controversial Innovation," *Teacher Education Quarterly*, 47 (1): 8–37.

Cochran-Smith, M., R. Jewett Smith, and J. Alexander (2022), "Mission, Money, and Membership: An Institutional Perspective on Teacher Preparation at New Graduate Schools of Education," *Education Policy Analysis Archives*, 30 (172). https://doi.org/10.14507/epaa.30.7500.

Cohen, J., V. Wong, A. Krishnamachari, and R. Berlin (2020), "Teacher Coaching in a Simulated Environment," *Educational Evaluation and Policy Analysis*, 42 (2): 208–31.

A Community of Inquiry (2018). *Keywords; for Further Consideration and Particularly Relevant to Academic Life, Especially as It Concerns Disciplines, Inter-Disciplinary Endeavor and Modes of Resistance to the Same*. Princeton: Princeton University Press.

Conway, Z. (2010), "Education 'revolution' in New Orleans." *BBC News*. April 8 . http://news.bbc.co.uk/2/hi/americas/8608960.stm.

Crawford-Garrett, K. (2013), *Teach for America and the Struggle for Urban School Reform: Searching for Agency in an Era of Standardization*, New York: Peter Lang.

Daniels, J. R., and M. Varghese (2019), "Troubling Practice: Exploring the Relationship Between Whiteness and Practice-Based Teacher Education in Considering a Raciolinguicized Teacher Subjectivity," *Educational Researcher*, 49 (1): 56–63.

Darling-Hammond, L. (2017), "Teacher Education Around the World: What Can We Learn from International Practice?," *European Journal of Teacher Education*, 40 (3): 291–309.

Darling-Hammond, L., D. Burns, C. Campbell, A. L. Goodwin, K. Hammerness, E. L. Low, A. McIntyre, M. Sato, and K. Zeichner (2017), *Empowered Educators: How Leading Nations Design Systems for Teaching Quality*, San Francisco: Jossey-Bass.

Davis, E., and T. Boerst (2014), "Designing Elementary Teacher Education to Prepare Well-Started Beginners," Working Paper, Ann Arbor, MI: TeachingWorks, University of Michigan School of Education.

Dresden, J., and K. F. Thompson (2021), "Looking Closely at Clinical Practice: A Clear-Eyed Vision for the Future of Teacher Education," *Peabody Journal of Education*, 96 (1): 8–21.

Dutro, E., and A. Cartun (2016), "Cut to the Core Practices: Toward Visceral Disruptions of Binaries in Practice-Based Teacher Education," *Teaching and Teacher Education*, 58: 119–28.

Ellis, V. (2010), "Impoverishing Experience: The Problem of Teacher Education in England," *Journal of Education for Teaching*, 36 (1): 105–20.

Ellis, V., and J. McNicholl (2015), *Transforming Teacher Education: Reconfiguring the Academic Work*, London: Bloomsbury.

Ellis, V., and J. Orchard (2014), "Learning Teaching 'from Experience': Towards a History of the Idea," in

V. Ellis and J. Orchard (eds.), *Learning Teaching from Experience: Multiple Perspectives and International Contexts*, 1–17, London: Bloomsbury.

Ellis, V., L. Gatti, and W. Mansell (2024), *The New Political Economy of Teacher Education: The Enterprise Narrative and the Shadow State*, Bristol: Policy Press.

Ellis, V., S. Steadman, and T. A. Trippestad (2019), "Teacher Education and the GERM: Policy Entrepreneurship, Disruptive Innovation and the Rhetorics of Reform," *Journal of Education Policy*, 31 (1): 101–21.

Ericsson, K. (2008), "Deliberate Practice and Acquisition of Expert Performance: A General Overview," *Academic Emergency Medicine*, (15): 988–94.

Ericsson, K. A., R. T. Krampe, and C. Tesch-Romer (1993). "The Role of Deliberate Practice in the Acquisition of Expert Performance," *Psychological Review*, 100 (3): 363–406.

Feiman-Nemser, S., and J. Remillard (1996), "Perspectives on Learning to Teach," in F. Murray (ed.), *The Teacher Educator's Handbook*, 63–91, San Francisco: Jossey-Bass.

Feiman-Nemser, S., and M. Buchmann (1985), "Pitfalls of Experience in Teacher Preparation," *Teachers College Record*, 87 (1): 53–65.

Fontdevila, C., A. Verger, A. Zancajo, and H. Jabbar (2025), "Taking Stock, Looking Ahead: New Developments and Approaches to Education Privatization and Marketization Research," in A. Zancajo, C. Fontdevila, H. Jabbar, and A. Verger (eds.), *Research Handbook on Education Privatization and Marketization*, 470–87, Cheltenham: Edward Elgar Publishing.

Forzani, F. M. (2014), "Understanding 'Core Practices' and 'Practice-Based' Teacher Education: Learning from the Past," *Journal of Teacher Education*, 65 (4): 357–68.

Furlong, J. (2023), "Universities, Research, and Initial Teacher Education in England and Wales: Taking the Long View," in I. Menter (ed.), *The Palgrave Handbook of Teacher Education Research*, 277–98, Oxford: Palgrave Macmillan.

Furlong, J., and M. Lawn, eds. (2011), *Disciplines of Education: Their Role in the Future of Education Research*, London: Routledge.

Furlong, J., L. Barton, S. Miles, C. Whiting, and G. Whitty (2000), *Teacher Education in Transition: Re-Forming Teacher Professionalism?*, Buckingham: Open University Press.

Gallie, W. B. (1955). "Essentially Contested Concepts," *Proceedings of the Aristotelian Society*, 56: 167–98.

Ganti, A. (2014), "Neoliberalism and Its Discontents: The Anthropology of Neoliberalism," *Annual Review of Anthropology*, 43: 89–104.

Gatti, L. (2019), "Learning to Teach in an Urban Teacher Residency," *Urban Education*, 54 (9): 1233–61.

Gatti, L., and T. Catalano (2015), "The Business of Learning to Teach: A Critical Metaphor Analysis of One Teacher's Journey," *Teaching and Teacher Education*, 45: 149–60.

Gawande, A. (2002), "The Learning Curve," *The New Yorker*, January 28.

Gist, C. D., M. Bianco, and M. Lynn (2019), "Examining Grow Your Own Programs across the Teacher Development Continuum: Mining Research on Teachers of Color and Nontraditional Educator Pipelines," *Journal of Teacher Education*, 70 (1): 13–25.

Givan, R., and A. Lang (2020), *Strike for the Common Good: Fighting for the Future of Public Education*, Ann Arbor: University of Michigan Press.

Givens, J. R. (2021), *Fugitive Pedagogy: Carter G. Woodson and the Art of Black Teaching*, Cambridge, MA: Harvard University Press.

Goodson, I. F. (1993), "Forms of Knowledge and Teacher Education," *Journal of Education for Teaching: JET Papers*, 19: 217–29.

Greene, M. (1997), "Teaching as Possibility: A Light in Dark Times," *Journal of Pedagogy, Pluralism, and Practice*, 1 (1): 14–24.

Greer, I., and V. Doellgast (2017), "Marketization, Inequality, and Institutional Change: Toward a New Framework for Comparative Employment Relations," *Journal of Industrial Relations*, 59 (2): 192–208.

Grossman, P. (2005), "Research on Pedagogical Approaches," in M. Cochran-Smith and K. M. Zeichner (eds.), *Studying Teacher Education*, 425–76, Mahwah, NJ: Lawrence Erlbaum.

Grossman, P. (2018), *Teaching Core Practices in Teacher Education*, Cambridge, MA: Harvard Education Press.

Grossman, P., and M. McDonald (2008), "Back to the Future: Directions for Research in Teaching and Teacher Education," *American Educational Research Journal*, 45 (1): 184–205.

Grossman, P., and U. Fraefel (2024), *Core Practices in Teacher Education: A Global Perspective*, Cambridge, MA: Harvard Education Press.

Grossman, P., C. Compton, D. Igra, M. Ronfeldt, E. Shahan, and P. W. Williamson (2009), "Teaching Practice: A Cross-Professional Perspective," *Teachers College Record*, 111 (9): 2055–100.

Grossman, P., M. Kavanagh, and C. G. Pupik Dean (2018), "Introduction," in P. Grossman (ed.), *Teaching Core Practices in Teacher Education*, 1–14, Cambridge, MA: Harvard Education Press.

Hammerness, K., K. Klette, I. S. Jenset, and E. T. Canrinus (2020), "Opportunities to Study, Practice, and Rehearse Teaching in Teacher Preparation: An International Perspective," *Teachers College Record*, 122 (11): 1–46.

Härmä, J. (2017), "Whose Children Go to Bridge International Academies? A School Choice for the Middle Class in Ijegun, Lagos," Gwarinpa, Abuja: ActionAid.

Hauser, M., and S. S. Kavanagh (2019), "Practice-Based Teacher Education," in G. W. Noblit (ed.), *Oxford Research Encyclopedia of Education*, Oxford: Oxford University Press.

Henry, K. L., and A. D. Dixson (2016), "'Locking the Door Before We Got the Keys': Racial Realities of the Charter School Authorization Process in Post-Katrina New Orleans," *Urban Education*, 51 (6): 617–44.

Hogan, A., and G. Thompson (2017), "Commercialisation in Education: Defining Key Terms," in *Oxford Research Encyclopedia of Education*, Oxford: Oxford University Press.

Holland, D., W. Lachicotte, D. Skinner, and C. Cain (1998), *Identity and Agency in Cultural Worlds*, Cambridge, MA: Harvard University Press.

Holmes Group (1990), *Tomorrow's Schools: Principles for the Design of Professional Development Schools: Executive Summary*, East Lansing, MI.

Hook, T. (2021), "Schooling as Plantation: Reproducing Racial Hierarchies in U.S. Public Education," *Comparative Education Review*, 65 (2): 217–38.

hooks, b. (1994), *Teaching to Transgress: Education as the Practice of Freedom*, New York: Routledge.

Horn, I. S., and B. D. Kane (2019), "What We Mean When We Talk about Teaching: The Limits of Professional

Language and Possibilities for Professionalizing Discourse in Teachers' Conversations," *Teachers College Record*, 121 (6): 1–32.

Jabbar, H. (2015), "'Every Kid Is Money': Market-Like Competition and School Leader Strategies in New Orleans," *Educational Evaluation and Policy Analysis*, 37 (4): 638–59.

Jabbar, H. (2016), "The Visible Hand: Markets, Politics, and Regulation in Post-Katrina New Orleans," *Harvard Educational Review*, 86 (1): 1–26.

Janssen, F., P. Grossman, and H. B. Westbroek (2015), "Facilitating Decomposition and Recomposition in Practice-Based Teacher Education: The Power of Modularity," *Teaching and Teacher Education*, 51 (October): 137–46.

Jenset, I. S., K. Klette, and K. Hammerness (2018), "Grounding Teacher Education in Practice Around the World: An Examination of Teacher Education Coursework in Teacher Education Program Documents," *Teaching and Teacher Education*, 70: 12–23.

Jones, B. M. A., and S. J. Ball, eds. (2023). *Neoliberalism and Education*. Education and Social Theory series. Abingdon: Routledge.

Kagan, M., and Y. Gez (2021), "'You'll Be Very Far from This Place': Temporal and Spatial Aspirations at Bridge International Academies in Kenya," *Critique of Anthropology*, 41 (4): 389–404.

Kavanagh, S. S., and K. A. Danielson (2020), "Practicing Justice, Justifying Practice: Toward Critical Practice Teacher Education," *American Educational Research Journal*, 57: 69–105.

Kennedy, M. M. (2016), "Parsing the Practice of Teaching," *Journal of Teacher Education*, 67 (1): 6–17.

Kennedy, M. M.. (1999), "The Role of Preservice Teacher Education," in L. Darling-Hammond and G. Sykes (eds.), *Teaching as the Learning Profession: Handbook of Policy and Practice*, 54–86, San Francisco: Jossey-Bass.

Kim, J. (2024), "Leading Teachers' Perspective on Teacher-AI Collaboration in Education," *Education and Information Technologies*, 29 (7): 8693–724.

Kirchgasler, K. M. (2016), "Teaching and Technology: Rethinking Educational Technology in a Neoliberal Era," *Educational Studies*, 52 (3): 217–34.

Klein, N. (2007), "The Shock Doctrine and the Marketization of Education," *Educational Policy*, 21 (3): 386–96.

Korthagen, F. A. J. (2010), "How Teacher Education Can Make a Difference," *Journal of Education for Teaching*, 36 (4): 407–23.

Korthagen, F. A. J., J. Kessels, B. Koster, B. Lagerwerf, and T. Wubbels (2001), *Linking Practice and Theory: The Pedagogy of Realistic Teacher Education*, Mahwah, NJ: Lawrence Erlbaum.

Kretchmar, K. (2014), "The Revolution Will Be Privatized: Teach For America and Charter Schools," *The Urban Review*, 46 (4): 632–53.

Kretchmar, K., and K. Zeichner (2016), "Teacher Prep 3.0: A Vision for Teacher Education to Impact Social Injustice," *Journal of Teacher Education*, 67 (4): 223–6.

Lampert, M. (2010), "Learning Teaching in, From, and for Practice: What Do We Mean?," *Journal of Teacher Education*, 61 (1–2): 21–34.

Lampert, M., M. L. Franke, E. Kazemi, H. Ghousseini, A. C. Turrou, H. Beasley, and K. Crowe (2013), "Keeping It Complex: Using Rehearsals to Support Novice Teacher Learning of Ambitious Teaching," *Journal of Teacher Education*, 64 (3): 226–43.

Lave, J. (1991), "Situating Learning in Communities of Practice," in L. B. Resnick, J. M. Levine, and S. D. Teasley (eds.) *Perspectives on Socially Shared Cognition*, 63–82, Washington, DC: American Psychological Association.

Lave, J. (2012), "Changing Practice," *Mind, Culture, and Activity*, 19 (2): 156–71.

Leary, J. P. (2018), *Keywords: The New Language of Capitalism*, New York: Routledge.

Leary, J. P. (2022), *Keywords for Capitalism: Power, Society, Politics*, Chicago: Haymarket Books.

Lemov, D. (2010), *Teach Like a Champion: 49 Techniques That Put Students on the Path to College (K–12)*, San Francisco: John Wiley & Sons.

Lemov, D. (2013), "From 'Professional' to 'Practice': Getting Better at Getting Better," *Pathway to Success*, Wisconsin Policy Research Institute.

Lemov, D. (2021), *Teach Like a Champion 3.0: 63 Techniques That Put Students on the Path to College*, San Francisco: John Wiley & Sons.

Lemov, D., E. Woolway, and K. Yezzi (2012), *Practice Perfect: 42 Rules for Getting Better at Getting Better*, San Francisco: Jossey-Bass.

Lewis, C. (2010), "Teachers and Teaching in Japan: Professional Mecca or Pressure Cooker?," in Y. Zhao, J. Lei, G. Li, M. F. He, K. Okano, N. Megahed, D. Gamage, and H. Ramanathan (eds.), *Handbook of Asian Education: A Cultural Perspective*, London: Routledge.

Lindberg, S., and Jonsson, A. (2023). "Preservice Teachers Training with Avatars: A Systematic Literature Review of 'Human-in-the-Loop' Simulations in Teacher Education and Special Education," *Education Sciences*, 13 (8): 817.

Lortie, D. C. (1975), *Schoolteacher: A Sociological Study*, Chicago: University of Chicago Press.

Love, B. L. (2019), *We Want to Do More Than Survive: Abolitionist Teaching and the Pursuit of Educational Freedom*, Boston: Beacon Press.

Lubienski, C. (2006), "School Choice and Privatization in Education: An Alternative Analytical Framework," *Journal for Critical Education Policy Studies*, 4 (1): 1–26.

Lubienski, C., and J. Malin (2025), "Market-Based Education Reforms and Their Global Impact," in A. Zancajo, C. Fontdevila, H. Jabbar, and A. Verger (eds.), *Research Handbook on Education Privatization and Marketization*, 26–40, Cheltenham: Edward Elgar Publishing.

Lund, K., and T. H. Eriksen (2016), "Teacher Education as Transformation: Some Lessons Learned from a Center for Excellence in Education," *Acta Didactica Norge*, 10 (2): 53–72.

Macpherson, I., S. Robertson, and G. Walford, eds. (2014), *Education, Privatisation and Social Justice: Case Studies from Africa, South Asia and South East Asia*, Providence, RI: Symposium Books.

Matsumoto-Royo, K., and M. S. Ramírez-Montoya (2021), "Core Practices in Practice-Based Teacher Education: A Systematic Literature Review of Its Teaching and Assessment Process," *Studies in Educational Evaluation*, 70: 1–13.

McCabe, C., H. Yanacek, and the Keywords Project (2018). *Keywords for Today. A 21st Century Vocabulary*, Oxford: Oxford University Press.

McDonald, M., E. Kazemi, and S. Kavanagh (2013), "Core Practices and Pedagogies of Teacher Education," *Journal of Teacher Education*, 64 (5): 378–86.

Menter, I., and M. Hulme (2012), "Teacher Education in Scotland – Riding Out the Recession?," *Educational Research*, 54 (2): 149–60.

Miron, G. (2008), "The Politics of Charter School Policy in the United States," *Education and Urban Society*, 40 (2): 180–206.

Mungal, A. S. (2016), "Teach For America, Relay Graduate School, and the Charter School Networks: The Making of a Parallel Education Structure," *Education Policy Analysis Archives*, 24 (17): 1–25.

National Academy of Education (2024), *Evaluating and Improving Teacher Preparation Programs*, K. M. Zeichner, L. Darling-Hammond, A. I. Berman, D. Dong, and G. Sykes (eds.), Washington, DC: National Academy of Education.

National Council for Accreditation of Teacher Education (NCATE) (2010), *Transforming Teacher Education through Clinical Practice: A National Strategy to Prepare Effective Teachers*, Washington, DC: NCATE.

Niemi, H., and R. Jakku-Sihvonen (2006), "Research-Based Teacher Education," in R. Jakku-Sihvonen and H. Niemi (eds.), *Research-Based Teacher Education in Finland: Reflections by Finnish Teacher Educators*, 31–50, Turku: Finnish Educational Research Association.

Offutt-Chaney, M. (2022), "'Black Crisis' and the 'Likely' Privatization of Public Education in New Orleans and Liberia," *Critical Studies in Education*, 63 (2), 180–95.

Organisation for Economic Co-operation and Development (OECD) (2012), *Public and private Schools: How Management and Funding Relate to Their Socio-Economic Profile*. OECD Publishing.

Organisation for Economic Co-operation and Development (OECD) (2019), *Trends Shaping Education 2019*, Paris: OECD Publishing.

Paris, D. and M. Winn (2013), *Humanizing Research: Decolonizing Qualitative Inquiry With Youth and Communities*, Los Angeles: Sage.

Paris, D., and H. S. Alim (2017), *Culturally Sustaining Pedagogies: Teaching and Learning for Justice in a Changing World*, New York: Teachers College Press.

Payne, K. A., L. Gatti, and K. Kretchmar (2025), "Recasting the Pitfalls of Experience in Teacher Preparation for the Current Context," *Teachers College Record*, 127 (3): 145–53.

Philip, T. M., M. Souto-Manning, L. Anderson, I. Horn, D. J. Carter Andrews, J. Stillman, and M. Varghese (2019), "Making Justice

Peripheral by Constructing Practice as 'Core': How the Increasing Prominence of Core Practices Challenges Teacher Education," *Journal of Teacher Education*, 70 (3): 251–64.

Plyer, A., N. Shrinath, and V. Mack (2015), *The New Orleans Index at Ten: Measuring Greater New Orleans' Progress Toward Prosperity*, New Orleans: The Data Center of Southeast Louisiana.

Reed, A. L., Jr. (2006), "Undone by Neoliberalism," *The Nation*, September 18.

Reid, J. (2011), A practice turn for teacher education?, *Asia-Pacific Journal of Teacher Education*, 39 (4): 293–310.

Riep, M. (2019a), "What Do We Know About Bridge International Academies? A Systematic Review of a Global Education Franchise," *Oxford Review of Education*, 45 (4): 463–80.

Riep, M. (2019b), *What Do We Know About Bridge International Academies? A Systematic Review of a Global Education Franchise*, Brussels: Education International Research.

Riep, M., and M. Machacek (2016), "Private Schooling in Low-Income Countries: Challenges and Opportunities," *Comparative Education Review*, 60 (4): 715–43.

Sahlberg, P. (2023), "Trends in Global Education Reform Since the 1990s: Looking for the Right Way," *International Journal of Educational Development*, 98: 102748.

Schierra, A. J. (2021), "Seeking Convergence and Surfacing Tensions Between Social Justice and Core Practices: Re-Presenting Teacher Education as a Community of Praxis," *Journal of Teacher Education*, 72 (4): 462–76.

Scribner, S., and M. Cole (1981), *The Psychology of Literacy*, Cambridge, MA: Harvard University Press.

Shulman, L. S. (1986), "Those Who Understand: Knowledge Growth in Teaching," *Educational Researcher*, 15 (2): 4–14.

Shulman, L. S. (1987), "Knowledge and Teaching: Foundations of the New Reform," *Harvard Educational Review*, 57 (1): 1–22.

Solomon, J. (2009), "The Boston Teacher Residency: District-Based Teacher Education," *Journal of Teacher Education*, 60 (5): 478–88.

Sondel, B. (2014), "Citizenship and the Politics of Market-Based School Reform," *Critical Questions in Education*, 5 (2): 109–25.

Sondel, B. (2015), "Raising Citizens or Raising Test Scores?: Teach For America, 'No Excuses' Charters, and the Development of the Neoliberal Citizen," *Theory and Research in Social Education*, 43 (3): 289–313.

Sondel, B. (2017), "(Re)Producing Neoliberal Citizens in a No Excuses Charter School," *Urban Education*, 52 (10): 1170–97.

Souto-Manning, M. (2019), "Transforming University-Based Teacher Education: Preparing Asset-, Equity-, and Justice-Oriented Teachers within the Contemporary Political Context," *Teachers College Record*, 121 (6): 1–29.

Souto-Manning, M., and J. Martell (2019), "Toward Critically Transformative Possibilities: Considering Tensions and Undoing Inequities in the Spatialization of Teacher Education," *Teachers College Record*, 121 (6): 1–42.

Srivastava, P. (2016), "Philanthropic Engagement in Education: Localised Expressions of Global Flows in India," *Contemporary Education Dialogue*, 13 (1): 5–32.

Steadman, S. (2018), "Defining Practice: Exploring the Meaning of Practice in the Process of Learning to Teach," *TEAN Journal*, 10 (1): 3–9.

Steiner-Khamsi, G. (2021), "Policy Borrowing and Lending in Comparative and International Education," in T. D. Jules, R. Shields, and M. A. M. Thomas (eds.), *The Bloomsbury Handbook of Theory in Comparative and International Education*, 329–46, London: Bloomsbury.

Stephens, L. (2013), *We Are the Face of Oaxaca: Testimony and Social Movements*, Durham, NC: Duke University Press.

Street, B. V. (2001), "Literacy Empowerment in Developing Societies," in *Literacy and Motivation*, 273–81, London: Routledge.

Swalwell, K., N. N. Rodríguez, A. Updegraff, and L. A. Winters (2023), "Distracting, Erasing, and Othering: A Critical Analysis of the Teachers Pay Teachers' Teach for Justice Collection," *Harvard Educational Review*, 93: 104–30.

Tyre, P. (2017), "Can a Tech Start-Up Successfully Educate Children in the Developing World?" *The New York Times Magazine*, June 27, 2017.

Varghese, M., J. R. Daniels, and C. C. Park (2019), "Structuring Disruption within University-Based Teacher Education Programs: Possibilities and Challenges of Race-Based Caucuses," *Teachers College Record*, 121 (6): 1–34.

Veltri, B. T. (2010), *Learning on Other People's Kids: Becoming a Teach for America Teacher*, Charlotte, NC: Information Age Publishing.

Verger, A., C. Fontdevila, and A. Zancajo (2016), *The Privatization of Education: A Political Economy of Global Education Reform*, New York: Teachers College Press.

Verger, A., C. Fontdevila, and A. Zancajo (2017), "Multiple Paths Towards Education Privatization in a Globalizing World: A Cultural Political Economy Review," *Education Finance and Policy*, 11 (2): 149–75.

Waslander, S., C. Pater and M. Van der Weide (2010), *Markets in Education: An Analytical Review of Empirical Research on Market Mechanisms in Education* (OECD Education Working Paper Series, No. 52). OECD Publishing.

White, T. (2016), "Teach for America's Paradoxical Diversity Initiative: Race, Policy, and Black Teacher Displacement in Urban Schools," *Education Policy Analysis Archives*, 24 (16): 1–37.

Whitty, G., J. Furlong, L. Barton, S. Miles, and C. Whiting (2007), *Teacher Education in Turmoil*, London: Open University Press.

Williams, R. (1976), *Keywords: A Vocabulary of Culture and Society*, London: Fontana Press.

Zancajo, A., C. Fontdevila, H. Jabbar, and A. Verger (2025), "Introduction: Education Privatization and Marketization in Global Perspective," in A. Zancajo, C. Fontdevila, H. Jabbar, and A. Verger (eds.), *Research Handbook on Education Privatization and Marketization*, 1–24, Cheltenham: Edward Elgar Publishing.

Zeichner, K. M. (2012), "The Turn Once Again Toward Practice-Based Teacher Education," *Journal of Teacher Education*, 63 (5): 376–82.

Zeichner, K. M. (2014), "The Struggle for the Soul of Teaching and Teacher Education in the USA," *Journal of Education for Teaching*, 40 (5): 551–68.

Zeichner, K. M. (2018), *The Struggle for the Soul of Teacher Education*, London: Routledge.

Zeichner, K. M. (2021), *Teacher Education and the Struggle for Social Justice*, 3rd ed., New York: Routledge.

Zeichner, K. M. (2023), *Keywords in Teacher Education: Community*, London: Bloomsbury.

Zeichner, K. M., and C. Peña-Sandoval (2015), "Venture Philanthropy and Teacher Education Policy in the U.S: The Role of the NewSchools Venture Fund," *Teachers College Record*, 117 (5): 1–44.

INDEX